CHILDREN OF DEPRESSED MOTHERS
From Early Childhood to Maturity

Children of Depressed Mothers provides a developmental perspective on the psychopathology of offspring of depressed mothers. A primary theme is the interplay of factors in the child (developmental stage, gender, temperament) and environment (depressed mother's symptomatic behavior and family functioning) as contributors to psychiatric and psychosocial problems in offspring. Children and their families are followed from toddlerhood to the threshold of adulthood. The emergence and evolution of problems differ by mother's diagnosis, whether unipolar or bipolar depressed or well. Configurations of variables in the individual child are identified that, in combination, create diverse processes that put offspring at risk for specific problems. Early depressed mother–child relationships are strongly influential. Specific affective and temperament qualities of mother and child act reciprocally, increasing risk. The longitudinal data grasp the nature of the connectedness of early experience to ongoing development, and identify patterns of child-to-adult connections. Findings suggest new questions and revised research paradigms.

Marian Radke-Yarrow is Research Scientist Emerita at the National Institute of Mental Health. From 1974 to 1995, she served as director of the Laboratory of Developmental Psychology, and her work has been honored with the G. Stanley Hall Award by the American Psychological Association and the award for Distinguished Scientific Contributions to Child Development Research by the Society for Research in Child Development.

CHILDREN OF
DEPRESSED MOTHERS

From Early Childhood
to Maturity

Marian Radke-Yarrow

in collaboration with
Pedro Martinez, Anne Mayfield,
and Donna Ronsaville

CAMBRIDGE
UNIVERSITY PRESS

PUBLISHED BY THE PRESS SYNDICATE OF THE UNIVERSITY OF CAMBRIDGE
The Pitt Building, Trumpington Street, Cambridge CB2 1RP, United Kingdom

CAMBRIDGE UNIVERSITY PRESS
The Edinburgh Building, Cambridge CB2 2RU, UK   http://www.cup.cam.ac.uk
40 West 20th Street, New York, NY 10011-4211, USA   http://www.cup.org
10 Stamford Road, Oakleigh, Melbourne 3166, Australia

Children of Depressed Mothers is the work of the Department of Health and Human
Services of the United States Government.

First published 1998

Printed in the United States of America

Typeset in Palatino 11/13.5 pt, in Penta[RF]

*A catalog record for this book is available from
the British Library*

Library of Congress Cataloging-in-Publication Data
Radke-Yarrow, Marian, 1918–

Children of depressed mothers: from early childhood to maturity /
Marian Radke-Yarrow, in collaboration with Pedro Martinez, Anne
Mayfield, and Donna Ronsaville.

p.   cm.

Includes bibliographical references   (p.).

ISBN 0-521-55131-5 (hardbound)

1. Children of depressed persons – Mental health.   2. Depression,
Mental – Etiology.   3. Mother and child.   4. Depressed persons –
Family relationships.   5. Child psychopathology – Longitudinal
studies.   I. Title.
RC537.R33   1998

616.85'27 – dc21   98-17213
                                                                            CIP

ISBN 0 521 55131 5 hardback

To all the families
who have struggled with depression

CONTENTS

PREFACE

This longitudinal study has a history that reflects the time in science at which it began, the research setting in which it was carried out, personal scientific interests and convictions, and the influence of colleagues. It is a study of the development of children of depressed parents.

The research focus is on the functioning of the parents and their children, particularly the affective texture of their interactions and relationships. Their behavior when alone and with each other, their subjective experiences, and the conditions of their lives are the data of the study.

A second focus is conceptual and methodological: There is richness in developmental theory, and sophistication in conceptualizations of behavioral processes. How can they be better incorporated into research practice?

For both themes, but especially the latter, the long ago mentorship of Kurt Lewin has had a permeating influence. His appreciation of the complexity of human behavior and development, and of the inseparability of person and environment, and his respect for the individual case are core orientations that enter into this study. His creative methodological approaches to social-affective problems, which were innovations in the research of the 1930s and 1940s, ring true in the 1990s. And I have borrowed from them. In his all but forgotten studies, *Autocracy and Democracy* (Lewin, Lippitt, & White, 1939) (which explored the effects of contrasting adult leadership styles on children's behavior) and *Frustration and Regression* (Barker, Dembo, & Lewin, 1941) (which examined the effects of unattainable goals on quality of child behavior), he created realistic experimental social–emotional situations in which children's behavior could be studied.

He demonstrated the art and science of experimental approaches to complex human behavior. The experiment as a method of investigating social–emotional processes is, he said, a powerful method, provided it retains the essence of the phenomena under study. A naturalistic experiment was not a contradiction. In the present study, we have used a blend of natural contexts with scripted conditions, and have tried to remain close to the essence of the phenomena.

The early research roots of the present study are in "normal" child development and "normal" families. Migration to psychopathology occurred gradually. The first step was an inquiry into the sensitivity of very young children to the affective states of other persons. Following Lewin's model, a naturalistic experiment was designed (with Phyllis Scott, 1965) to observe the responses of three-year-olds to small incidents in which an adult or child expressed emotional distress. These incidents were woven into nursery school activities. For example, a teacher might bump her head and wince as she picked up toys from under a table. Or, a telephone call might leave tears and sadness on the face of the adult. These events not only registered with the three-year-olds but elicited diverse reactions.

Two research questions followed naturally: When, in development, did these sensitivities emerge? How might chronic affective qualities of persons (sadness, fear, anger) – especially of parents – influence children? For answers, it was necessary to take the research into the family and to enlist mothers' help in observing children's reactions to natural and staged emotional events and interactions (Yarrow & Waxler, 1978). These studies were persuasive in showing the strong effects on young children of the affective qualities of their environments.

At the time of these studies, the National Institute of Mental Health, where the preceding research had been conducted, had as its priority investigation of "the major mental illnesses," of which affective disorder was one. This priority and a research interest in children's affective development had common ground.

The direction and substance of the research changed greatly in this union. Research on psychopathology and developmental processes called for a collaboration of disciplines. The clinical expertise of psychiatry was one essential. The developmental orientation and knowledge and the methodological skills of developmental psychology furnished the other essential.

The two disciplines brought different perspectives to the research: what do we want to learn? How should children be assessed? How important is the variable of development? How adequate are the diagnostic labels applied to children? Psychiatric interviews and behavioral observations do not tell the same story. Which are more valid? How important is context or environment in interpreting a child's behavior? Developmental psychologists and child psychiatrists worked together, gathering a rich body of data on the children and the parents, and progressively and successfully capitalized on the strengths of the two disciplines.

The longitudinal approach provided opportunities for methodological explorations – challenging usual ways of sampling behavior, drawing upon multiple data sources, investigating environment developmentally, and bringing individual differences and intraindividual processes onto the same stage. Observation of affectively ill and psychiatrically well parents and their children has permitted exploration of the interface of normal and psychopathological processes.

There is a danger, when research is focused on psychopathology, that normal development and mental health are seen only in terms of difference from psychopathology. The normal and well lose their identity. Although ill and well do not get equal consideration in this research, both receive attention in their own right.

The credo of developmental theorists for a long time has been that child behavior and development are multidetermined in interactional processes. In the present study, the broad base of empirical data on the parents, families, and children allows us to investigate multiple influences and interactive processes. The longitudinal approach also permits us to consider causal processes.

This report brings the children to adolescence and early adulthood, but the study goes on, as our "children" mature. Their life course is being followed into adulthood.

ACKNOWLEDGMENTS

This research has been nurtured by the participation and support of many colleagues. I gratefully and warmly acknowledge their contributions and express my thanks. In the early phases of the study and in the first stages of data collection, Michael Chapman, Leon Kuczynski, and Carolyn Zahn-Waxler played vital roles. Through the sensitive and caring work of Anne Mayfield, Anna Polissar, and Judy Stilwell, the families were introduced to the study and learned to know and trust the research enterprise. In the formative stages of instrument and procedural construction, development of coding schemes, and early analyses of data, Barbara Belmont became the manager and "memory" for all things in the study. Her work continued over 12 years. In the early period of the study, Leon Cytryn and Donald McKnew provided invaluable clinical experience and expertise in developing and testing measures of the youngest participants, the toddlers. Tracy Sherman Yaffe and Sarah Friedman also made valuable contributions to the conceptualizations and strategies guiding analyses of the youngest children. For his help in shaping the later psychiatric assessments of the children and parents, I express my thanks to Gerald Brown.

As the study and the children "aged," questions and methods were tuned to take account of children's changing developmental needs. In this process, other investigators joined the research for varying periods of time, bringing creative ideas and energies to the study: Grazyna Kochanska, Editha Nottelmann, Mark Cummings, John Richters, Elbert Wilson, Marybeth Fox, Frances Bridges-Cline, Gale Inoff-Germain, Kathleen Free, Pedro Martinez, Elizabeth DeMulder, Louisa Tarullo, Eurnestine Brown, Giovanna Municchi, and Bonnie Klimes-Dougan. All carried responsibilities for the development of procedures, data collection, supervision of technical assistants, and writing scientific reports. The contributions of Pedro Martinez are many. I deeply appreciate his careful supervision of the clinical assessments, his work on the clinical analyses, and his sensitive feedback to the parents.

Other colleagues and students came into the study briefly to investigate specific questions for which the data base of the study provided a ready-made data source: Zvia Breznitz, Wendy Habelow, Dale Hay, David Pelligrini, Serge Stoleru, Elizabeth Sussman, Elizabeth Tingley, Ruth Wylie, and Carolyn Zahn-Waxler. Their scientific reports have added to our knowledge of depressed mothers and their children.

The core raw data of the study are the audio/video records, year after year, of the children and their parents. I especially thank Paul Jordan for his help and advice on all aspects of this work. I am very indebted to him for video records of superb quality. As the data base grew in size and complexity, the job of data management grew likewise. The expertise and dedication of Jean Welsh made this a model in management. To her, I express special appreciation. Shizuko Ogata's work as librarian for this research made her a valued contributor for many years. Throughout much of the early phases of the study, I gratefully depended on John Bartko as statistical advisor. For bringing their expertise and energies to some of the difficult problems of analysis, thanks go to Dorothy Richardson and Kathleen McCann. For her statistical expertise and tireless labors in the integrative phase of the study, the contributions of Donna Ronsaville have been vital to the research.

There are many, many students and research assistants who have entered into the study, in the hard work of administering procedures, coding data, and processing and analyzing data. Although their labors cannot be individually recognized, they are much appreciated.

For accomplishing the countless complex tasks of readying the manuscript, I am indebted to Jean Mayo. Thanks also go to Alicia Green for her assistance on graphics.

I return to express thanks and affection to Anne Mayfield, who has been with the study from its beginning. She has been the durable, creative, and energetic member of the staff to whom the families and the research staff turned for help and understanding.

Most of all, much is owed to the families who have given so much of their time to the research. Because of their generous cooperation and dedication, it has been possible to study development over the span of childhood.

The steady support of the National Institute of Mental Health has made a longitudinal study possible. I wish to recognize especially the administration of John Eberhart and Robert Cohen for giving both tangible and intangible support to the launching of this study in 1979. Also, over a decade (1982–92), the John D. and Catherine T. MacArthur Foundation provided continuing additional support. I express my deep appreciation and thanks.

Marian Radke-Yarrow

1
ORIENTATION AND THEMES

The night was long and cold as I sat alone in the vast darkness, alone in my own world, my own frame of mind. I have traveled through great lands without leaving my room. I have felt the pain of a great many people, although I was never comforted through my storms. I have heard the feelings of many others, although my cries fell on deaf ears. I have wiped the tears of many, yet my face still ran wet. I have watched others stand tall on the glory that should have been mine. I have expressed my feelings, only to have them thrown back at me in a whirl of hatred. I have trusted, only to find out that there is no real meaning to the word. But most of all I loved, only to be made to feel unwanted and unloved. I have called each and every by name only to be called . . . DEPRESSION.

> Alice, 14 years, the daughter of a mother with bipolar illness

Many children grow up with a depressed parent. Many of these children develop serious problems – often depression – sometime in their lives. The nature of this passage of parental psychopathology to offspring psychopathology, which remains a puzzle in many respects, is the subject of this research.

Evidence from many studies leads to the generally accepted conclusion that both genetic and environmental factors are involved. What is not clear is how these factors, together, influence the transmission of depression from parent to offspring.

Because depression appears at elevated rates among relatives and across generations, it is assumed that children of depressed parents are at risk for depression. Depressed parents, then, have become the temporary "stand-ins" for genetic risk. Parents are also the "carriers" of potential environmental risks through their impaired functioning and the disordered conditions and relationships in their families. The parents, as environments for their children, are a primary focus in this study.

Investigations into genetic and environmental mechanisms in depression have generally proceeded as quite separate lines of research. Although only partial explanations can result from this separation, detailed analyses within each domain are necessary steps toward a more comprehensive understanding of the interdependent contributions of both domains.

THE STUDY

The focus of this study is on the course of offspring development and the factors influencing development. The children and their environments have been followed from the early years of childhood to the threshold of adulthood. Alice's depression has a history; she has lived her entire childhood with depressed parents. Her developmental path is one of coping and of vulnerability in the face of parental depression.

Depression takes a heavy toll on intrapersonal well-being. It invades many aspects of functioning – mood disturbances, changes in feelings of self-worth, disturbed sleep and appetite, psychomotor agitation or retardation, disturbed thought processes, reduced or exaggerated energy, decreased interest, hopelessness, and decreased feelings of pleasure. These qualities of life not only bring intrapersonal distress, they also affect the interpersonal functioning and relationships of the depressed person. The symptoms of depression and their consequences intrude into the lives of persons close by. The child of a depressed parent is "close by" over a long period of time and, with certainty, experiences the parent's illness.

Alice knows that her mother is ill. She has known for a long time. Her grandmother explained it to her when her mother was taken to the hospital. But it doesn't help her to stop crying some nights, to keep her mind on her work in school, to make her less anxious about what her mother might say or do when her friends come to the house, to forget her mother's degrading words about her sister and herself – "children are good for nothing but trouble," or to take away the heavy hopelessness she feels. Was she going to be like her mother? Was life only going to get worse?

Because depression can be profoundly inclusive in its cognitive and behavioral impairments, the impact of parental depression on the child may be felt across an extremely broad span of functions, over a long period of time. Therefore, inquiry into the transmission of depression must be concerned with the child's experiences and functioning over time – the lifetime of the child.

PLACE IN THE FIELD

This study comes to a research field that is crowded with many studies of depressed parents and their offspring. However, the present research enters this field where there has been the least investigation: (1) It is a prospective, long-term longitudinal study. (2) It imposes a developmental perspective on psychopathology, referenced to normal developmental processes. (3) It examines the development of the children of depressed and well mothers in context, namely, in the behavioral environments provided by their mothers and families. In this sense, it is a longitudinal study of parenting by depressed mothers, and a longitudinal description of functioning and survival of families in the face of chronic parental depression. (4) It provides the kinds of data necessary to investigate processes underlying offspring development.

The research literature is reviewed in chapter 3, but a brief overview of the field at this point provides context for the orientation and objectives of the study.

In many of the early studies, the offspring were adults when assessments were made of their psychiatric status – when psychopathology appeared at elevated rates, compared with rates in offspring of nondepressed parents. Children made their way into offspring studies by several routes. The theoretical possibility, and

3

later the demonstration, of depression in childhood stimulated work in this area. Then, too, studies of children of schizophrenic mothers included children of depressed mothers as comparison groups, only to find that they, too, showed troubling impairments.

Initially, psychiatry and developmental psychology contributed relatively independently to the research on children. Psychiatry brought the diagnostic system used in classifying adult disorders to the assessment of children, thus providing a standard measurement framework, but a somewhat static and nondevelopmental view of the child. Developmental psychologists evaluated children's cognitive and psychosocial functioning, sometimes adding psychiatric diagnostic assessments, again mainly nondevelopmentally. Psychiatric studies concentrated on older children; developmental psychologists, on infants and young children.

As the field expanded, the research focus broadened, from questions regarding the rates of offspring problems to questions of factors influencing the rates. Interestingly, psychiatrists, psychologists, and sociologists directed most of their attention to family functioning and family stress. The intimate interdependencies of depressed parents and offspring in their daily lives received much less attention.

Most research on maternal depression and offspring psychopathology has been cross-sectional, or follow-up studies spanning only a few years, or retrospective accounts. The literature is without prospective, long-term longitudinal studies.

Nevertheless, the existing body of research is the primer for the present study, providing provocative findings, leaving many questions unanswered, and raising new questions.

CONCEPTUAL ORIENTATION

The study draws on a history of theoretical writings in psychology that emphasize the complexity of individual development. Whether from a psychoanalytic, child development, or neurochemical perspective, behavioral development is viewed as a pro-

4

cess involving multiple influences. Over the years, theorists of widely varied backgrounds, in a common voice, have called for formulations of research problems and use of methods that incorporate this complexity.

In 1931, Kurt Lewin's formulation of behavior as a function of person and environment eloquently emphasized the interaction of systems within the person and within the environment, and the embeddedness of individual behavior in multiple and overlapping contexts. Barker (1968) carried Lewinian theory into "ecological psychology," drawing attention to how much child behavior was studied without reference to the contexts in which it occurred. Bronfenbrenner (1979) furthered this awareness by developing a conceptual scheme for systematically considering contextual information at multiple levels. In 1951, Sears advocated the mother–child dyad as a unit of analysis to replace sole reliance on data in which the child is viewed in isolation. In 1968, Bell published an influential paper in which he argued for consideration of the mutual, bidirectional child–parent influences on the behavior of both. Sameroff and Chandler (1975), Cairns (1986), Cicchetti and Aber (1986), and Rutter (1989a, b), among others, have stressed multiple interactional processes between child and environment. Hinde (1979) introduced more complexity by focusing on the importance of networks of relationships influencing individual behavior. Magnusson and Bergman (1988) concisely summarize these orientations:

> Development is regarded as a *process* in which cognitive-affective and biological factors in the individual, and distal and proximal factors in the environment are involved in a constant reciprocal interaction. (p. 47)

These formulations provide a challenging theoretical–conceptual framework for the present study, one that is relevant to the research objectives of understanding the development of children of depressed parents, as a group and in their individuality. An overriding challenge in this formulation lies in conceptualizing and measuring the behavioral environment.

5

DEVELOPMENT IN ENVIRONMENTAL CONTEXT

Individual development is inextricably bound up with the environment in which it is embedded. Both child and environment are changing along interrelated paths and by interrelated processes. The individual's behavior is both consequence and context. To capture person–environment interdependencies, we have undertaken a detailed study of the behavioral environment (Wachs, 1983; Radke-Yarrow, 1991), focusing on the proximal day-to-day surroundings of the child: (1) the behavior of the depressed mother, (2) the actions and interactions of family members, and (3) the attributes that the child brings to mother and family. (This is not to minimize influences of more distal environmental factors.) As much as possible, the environment is assessed in behavioral terms, on a par in specificity with assessment of the child. Each of these components is comprised of many variables. Each, too, in unspecified ways, is expressive of the genetic background of parents and offspring.

Maternal depression is the main "independent" variable throughout the study. Clearly, it is not a homogeneous condition with respect to etiology, history, or behavioral expression. We are interested in learning how these differences (with the emphasis on behavioral expression) make a difference for the offspring. The family contexts of interactions, relationships, and conditions too, vary in strains and supports. How do they impact on the child? Offspring bring individual predispositions and qualities into the interactions. How do these variables alter family responses to the offspring and also affect offspring responses to maternal depression?

These environmental components are "separate" only conceptually. We assume that they do not act separately on the child. We look to configurations of environmental variables – coexisting and sequential – for additive, synergistic, and interactive impact on the child. The environment has holistic characteristics with effects that may be at variance with findings of effects based on single dimensions.

6

If we step back, for a moment, from the specific content of maternal depression, it is at once apparent that we are investigating a very old question. In generic terms, it is a search for processes through which parents (families) influence their children's development. There is knowledge to be applied in this study from the much-studied field of "normal" development. From it, we have learned the importance of the child's maturational level in affecting the child's openness and vulnerability to environmental influences. The critical role of timing in determining the consequences of experiences has been repeatedly documented. The early years have been stressed as creating or potentiating vulnerabilities that persist in development. Much responsibility is placed on the caregiver for providing the child with the security, management, and support needed for adaptive development. No less, the negative influences of discordant and disrupted family relationships and, contrariwise, the positive influences of congenial, supportive family relationships have been documented in research. Also, developmental research provides information on mechanisms through which adults influence children (e.g., social reinforcement, modeling). Are they useful frameworks in which to view depressed mothers' influences? Comparisons of psychopathological environments and healthy environments in interaction with high- and low-risk children should be informative with regard to same and different underlying processes.

SUMMARY

Our data are detailed accounts, over time, of the behavioral development and the behavioral environment of children of depressed and well parents. We investigate the transmission of psychopathology and adaptation from parent to child, through the interaction of person and environmental factors. We anticipate multiple processes and multiple outcomes.

The inherently complicated components present considerable challenge to the methods of research. The phenomena of interest can be lost (Cairns, 1986) at any step in the research process – in the data gathered, the transformations of raw data into concepts and categories, and the statistical approaches. We have tried to be aware of, and to deal with, these difficulties. We take heart and proceed, encouraged by Robert Hinde's (1988b) prediction that "somewhere behind all this complexity, waiting to be revealed, is orderliness" (p. 3).

2

AN OVERVIEW

Because a longitudinal study is a long and complicated story, we begin with an overview of the study structure as a guide. The details are elaborated in the later chapters.

This is a study of children growing up, from toddlerhood to late adolescence and young adulthood. The children are offspring of unipolar and bipolar depressed mothers and offspring of psychiatrically well parents. It is a study of the psychiatric and psychosocial development of children in these contrasting conditions of risk, and the factors contributing to children's development.

The study takes its form from the theoretical orientation and conceptualizations described in the preceding chapter: Behavior and development are viewed as complex and multidetermined, and research design and procedures are geared to respect these properties.

The research approach is longitudinal in order to observe the child's problems through time, in relation to the stable and changing contexts in which behavior is embedded. The band of data obtained on the child and the environmental contexts is broad, in order to measure multiple, interrelated influences and consequences.

Assessments of children's functioning include dimensions of self-regulatory behavior, affect expression and regulation, cognitive functioning, attitudes toward self, and interpersonal relationships. Assessments of the proximal behavioral environments of family and parent behavior are likewise of many dimensions of person and interpersonal characteristics, at macro- and micro-levels and at consecutive periods of development.

Many objectives converge in the goal of understanding offspring development in the context of maternal depression. The mechanisms through which depression is transmitted to the offspring are of special interest, but attention is not focused exclusively on depression as an outcome. The broader question is one of individual development. When do specific problems emerge and how do they evolve in childhood? What are the factors, external and internal to the child, that, in interaction, influence the development of specific maladaptive and adaptive patterns of behavior? It is in these terms that the specific outcomes of depression can best be understood.

Because the study is focused predominantly on risks and problems, healthy development tends to be the absence of pathology. Indeed, our well mothers were selected on absence of parental psychopathology and severe family dysfunction, not by characteristics specifically predictive of adaptive or optimal offspring development. Factors that are protective or facilitative of children's development are not ignored and indeed they are illuminating in understanding risks. The psychiatrically well parents and their children allow us to examine differences in ill and well families that are not only descriptive but that help to identify possible differences in parent-to-child transmission processes in normal and psychopathological development.

Analyses proceed in a variety of ways with varied objectives: In initial cross-sectional analyses, we describe children of mothers with major depression, bipolar illness, or no psychiatric diagnosis, at successive stages of development, on their patterns of psychiatric and psychosocial problems. The data in these analyses do not deal with processes, although they may suggest a direct genetic link between parent diagnosis and child status.

The data are analyzed longitudinally to compare the course of development of the children of the three maternal diagnostic groups and to describe the course of development of the individual child. The analyses allow us to investigate the emergence and evolution of specific kinds of problems and comorbidities of problems. The analyses reveal the diversity in developmental course within each maternal diagnosis as well as across maternal diagnostic groups.

Questions regarding mechanisms of transmission drive the next stages of analysis. We look first to variables within the mother's diagnosis to interpret differences in children's outcomes. Do characteristics of mothers' illness affect offspring development? Are family histories of affective disorders related to offspring problems?

Factors of family functioning, depressed mother–child relationships, and child characteristics introduce substantial differences and complexity. How do these multiple factors, singly and in patterns, shape the child's involvement with the mother's depression and influence the child's functioning? Progressively we shift attention and analyses to multiple interacting influences on offspring outcomes. We examine subgroups of offspring who are homogeneous in patterns of characteristics to pursue the possibility of identifying specific configurations that generate processes linking maternal depression to offspring psychopathology.

3

QUESTIONS AND ANSWERS IN THE LITERATURE

Research on clinically depressed parents and their children has generated numerous comprehensive reviews (Orvaschel, Weissman, & Kidd, 1980; Beardslee, Bemporad, Keller, & Klerman, 1983; Downey & Coyne, 1990; Gelfand & Teti, 1990; Goodman, 1992; Cummings & Davis, 1994), evidence of the scientific interest in the topic. Hundreds of studies of parental depression and associated offspring problems have appeared in the research literature.

We have not undertaken an inclusive review of this research. We have, instead, imposed on the literature the specific questions and issues that concern us in this study, namely, the course of offspring development and the conditions or factors associated with the development of, or "escape" from, psychopathology. First, however, we review the reviews for the general state of the field. (This review does not include research on genetic mechanisms.)

A major signpost in reviews is the elevated rate of problems in the offspring. Epidemiological and clinical studies (reviewed in Beardslee et al., 1983) have repeatedly brought out the differences in rates of disorders in the offspring of depressed versus nondepressed parents. Geneticists, through family studies and twin and adoption studies, have provided strong evidence of genetic transmission (e.g., Nurnberger, Goldin, & Gershon, 1986). Other research has implicated environmental factors as contributors to the links between parent and offspring psychopathologies (e.g., Emery, Weintraub, & Neale, 1982). Most investigators speak in broad terms of genetic–environmental interaction. A genetic contribution is necessary, but not sufficient, to explain the findings (Rutter, MacDonald, Le Couteur, Harrington, Bolton, & Bailey, 1990; Lombroso, Pauls, & Leckman, 1995).

Although there is repeated confirmation of elevated rates of

12

problems in offspring of depressed parents, the frequency, kinds, and seriousness of reported problems differ from study to study. The ubiquity of the overall finding is remarkable, given the heterogeneity within the diagnosis of depression, the methodological failings in early studies (e.g., lack of comparison groups, "softness" in specifications of parental diagnoses as well as child problems), and varied criteria of assessment.

The persistence of the parent–offspring link has pressed the question of mechanisms. When Downey and Coyne wrote their comprehensive review in 1990, of what by then had become a vast psychological and psychiatric literature, they could go well beyond the declaration of risk to offspring. Research had developed in several distinct directions. Many studies dealt with the effects of parental depression specifically on children. Other studies were concerned with the effects of conditions correlated with parental depression, especially disturbed family life. Other studies focused on depressed mothers' impaired functioning in the parent role, emphasizing the carry-over of symptoms of illness into interactions with their children. However, studies were rarely designed to consider, together, maternal diagnosis, maternal functioning, and family variables as factors influencing offspring.

Downey and Coyne's review provides a critique as well as a review of the research. They point out that investigators have given little attention to heterogeneity within the diagnosis of depression and have been insufficiently specific regarding children's problems. Are their problems different from the problems of children of other parental-risk groups? How far has research been able to disentangle effects of parental depression from the effects of correlated stressful conditions? How have intergenerational pathologies been explained? In brief, their review exposed the complexity of parental depression and offspring problems, and brought further pressure on the field to consider processes of transmission. Downey and Coyne conclude that "adequate explanatory models must incorporate considerable complexity."

Reviewers like Downey and Coyne and also Goodman (1992) seem especially eager for shifts in research emphases. They are wanting more, and hypothesizing more, than the existing empirical literature has to give. Cummings and Davis (1994), too, are thinking ahead of the research evidence. Their discussion draws on normal child development and socialization research as sources of theory and suggestions for future research. Processes of modeling, reinforcement, cognitive processing, and attachment are placed in the context of depressed mothering, and inferences are drawn concerning the operation of these mechanisms when a mother is depressed. The validity of their speculations rests on the assumption that linkage mechanisms are identical in normal and psychopathological development. These reviewers conclude, therefore, that what has been found in studies of normal development *may* be applicable in interpreting the influences of depression on children, but the relevant research on maternal depression has not been done.

The many studies that have entered into the reviews have one overriding characteristic. They are cross-sectional or follow-ups over short periods of time. Conspicuously absent is systematic investigation of development as a variable affecting the impact of maternal depression on offspring. Long-term longitudinal studies in which it is possible to observe development through important life phases are not in the reviews.

QUESTIONS FOR RESEARCH

The wealth of research on depression has produced a strong foundation and stimulus for continuing research on questions that are raised by the findings, but are not fully answered. We now raise the questions and review the evidence that is relevant for the present study.

WHAT ARE THE DEVELOPMENTAL CHARACTERISTICS OF OFFSPRING OF DEPRESSED MOTHERS?

Many characteristics of offspring have been studied. Many kinds of impairments have been reported. Cognitive ability, information

14

processing, and academic performance were among the variables in early assessments of offspring impairments (e.g., Cohler, Grunebaum, Weiss, Gamer, & Gallant, 1977; Billings & Moos, 1983; Weissman, Gammon, John, Merikangas, Warner, Prusoff, & Sholomskas, 1987). Impairments in social competencies and peer relationships were found by Weintraub, Prinz, and Neale (1978); Jaenicke, Hammen, Zupan, Hiroto, Gordon, Adrian, and Burge (1987); Goodman and Brumley (1990); and others. Negative self-image is reported by Jaenicke et al. (1987). Disturbances in infant affect, (e.g., Field, 1984) and disturbed early attachment relationships (e.g., Radke-Yarrow, Cummings, Kuczynski, & Chapman, 1985; Crittenden, 1988) add to the list of impairments.

Increasingly, studies have focused on psychiatric diagnoses of children. Significantly more children of unipolar depressed parents than children of normal controls are reported to have diagnoses (Weissman, Prusoff, Gammon, Merikangas, Leckman, & Kidd, 1984; Keller, Beardslee, Dorer, Lavori, Samuelson, & Klerman, 1986; Weissman et al., 1987; Orvaschel, Walsh-Allis, & Ye, 1988; Hammen, 1991). Affective disturbances (major depression as well as less severe depressive signs) distinguish children of unipolar depressed parents from children of normal control parents in the reports of Welner, McCrary, and Leonard (1977); Weissman et al. (1987); Klein, Clark, Dansky, and Margolis (1988); and Orvaschel et al. (1988). Significantly higher rates of affective disturbances appear also in the offspring of bipolar parents (e.g., Decina, Kestenbaum, Farber, Kron, Gargan, Sackheim, & Fieve, 1983; Klein, Depue, & Slater, 1985).

Is it possible from these many studies to derive developmental profiles of when given problems emerge, become most prevalent, or recede? It is not. Information is available on different ages on different problems. Within studies, offspring often represent a wide range of ages (from prepubertal to postpubertal years, from early school age to adulthood). Some problems have been studied primarily at a single developmental period. For example, distorted affect and difficulties in regulation of affect have been a focus in studies of infancy and toddlerhood (e.g., Field, 1984; Gaensbauer, Harmon, Cytryn, & McKnew, 1984; Zahn-Waxler, McKnew, Cum-

15

mings, Davenport, & Radke-Yarrow, 1984; Cohn, Matias, Tronick, Connell, & Lyons-Ruth, 1986; Cox, Puckering, Pound, & Mills, 1987). In studies of school-age children (6 to 16), there is a concentration on diagnoses (e.g., Cytryn, McKnew, Bartko, Lamour, & Hamovit, 1982; Decina et al., 1983; Orvaschel et al., 1988; Lee & Gotlib, 1989; Hammen, 1991).

Age is given relatively little serious attention as an informative variable. The fact that problems of one type or another have been found at whatever age is studied has possibly minimized interest in age as a variable. Given that parental influence on the child is, itself, a developmental question, it is ironic that development as a variable has had so little attention in the research.

WHAT IS THE EVIDENCE ON THE COURSE OF INDIVIDUAL DEVELOPMENT IN CHILDREN OF DEPRESSED MOTHERS?

This question shifts the focus to the individual. It is curious that there has not been greater research interest in the continuity and discontinuity of problems in individual offspring. Do problems come and go, persist, change over time? Is there a common path of problem development? Are there given developmental periods of greatest vulnerability? Are certain kinds of experiences, at given periods, especially "lethal"? How robust are the links between problems in the early years and outcomes in adolescence and adulthood? Are there specific precursors of later problems? There is little research information on most of these questions.

Although many studies have longitudinal, follow-up, or follow-back components, they cover limited sections of development. In longitudinal studies spanning the preschool period, children of depressed parents show more impairments than children of control mothers in repeated assessments (e.g., Goodman, 1992). Follow-up studies of the school years (sometimes beginning in preschool) also report relatively constant differences between depressed and control groups at initial and follow-up assessments (e.g., Cohler et al., 1977; Richman, Stevenson, & Graham, 1982;

16

Lee & Gotlib, 1989; Garrison & Earls, 1985; Hammen, 1991). But from these studies, we do not learn whether the same children are having continuing problems.

The large-sample community studies in which children's problems are assessed at repeated intervals over a number of years could help us here. They provide the kind of data on children that are needed; namely, intraindividual consistencies over time, temporal ordering of problems, and patterns of problems. But unfortunately these studies do not have information on parent diagnostic characteristics (e.g., Ledingham & Schwartzman, 1984).

Overall, information is scanty with regard to the individual course of psychopathological development in offspring of depressed mothers.

DO DIFFERENCES IN THE CHARACTERISTICS OF PARENTS' DEPRESSION AND IN FAMILY PSYCHIATRIC HISTORY MAKE A DIFFERENCE IN OFFSPRING OUTCOMES?

There are many investigations relating to this question. Parental depression varies in etiology, course, severity, and symptomatology. One or both parents may be depressed. Families vary in histories of affective illness among their relatives.

Severity and Chronicity

A study by Keller et al. (1986) confirmed what might be anticipated, that greater severity and chronicity of parents' illness is significantly positively associated with greater impairment and more frequent diagnoses (DSM-III) in the children. The significant associations are modest (rank correlations ranging from .23 to .38). The findings are supported, however, in other studies (Harder, Kokes, Fisher, & Strauss, 1980; Hammen, Adrian, Gordon, Burge, Jaenicke, & Hiroto, 1987; Klein et al., 1988). On the other hand, Orvaschel et al. (1988) found no relation between number of epi-

17

sodes and Hamilton ratings of severity of maternal depression and frequencies of child psychopathology. To the extent that severity and chronicity mean greater exposure of the child to parental symptoms, greater impact on the child is a reasonable expectation. Alternative processes may also be operating: Severity may be an indicator of etiological factors that carry more risk.

Episode and Interepisode Functioning

Studies of maternal functioning between major depressive episodes raise interesting questions. Rutter and Quinton (1984), reporting on the course of parental illness over a 4-year period, found that few parent patients were symptom-free between episodes. These authors stress the persistence of parental symptoms as having the impact on children. Other investigators, too, have confirmed that the intervals between episodes generally involve continuities in impaired parental behavior (Weissman & Paykel, 1974; Harder et al., 1980; Billings & Moos, 1985; Lee & Gotlib, 1991; Stein, Gath, Bucher, Bond, Day, & Cooper, 1991).

Which pattern of maternal functioning is more difficult for children – maternal functioning that is punctuated by depressive episodes of dysfunction followed by symptom-free behavior, or maternal behavior that is dysfunctional more or less continuously over time with accented dysfunction in episodes? The data from Billings and Moos (1985), Lee and Gotlib (1991), and Stein et al. (1991) indicate that child adjustment does not fluctuate significantly as the parent moves in and out of episodes, thereby suggesting that it is the continuing experiences in mother–child interaction and relationships and/or the persistence of maternal dysfunction that have the greater impact on the child's adaptation.

It would be helpful to learn how children react to the mother when she is in an acute episode or is exhibiting severely symptomatic behavior, compared with when her behavior is normal. Such data are difficult to obtain, however, at least directly. How children cope with an episode of depression or mania, and how the mother's extreme behavior is processed cognitively, are areas virtually untouched by research.

18

Personality Disorder and Depression

Personality disorders frequently occur with depression. Personality or personality disorder is understood to be the relatively enduring characteristic of the individual, in which case it may well be that persistent maternal dysfunction between major episodes of depression reflects the enduring presence of personality disorders. In the few studies in which personality disorders have been investigated, they appear to be risks for offspring problems. Cooper, Leach, Storer, and Tonge (1977) reported that psychiatric risk to children was increased when the mother had a personality disorder. Rutter and Quinton (1984) reported a similar finding. The findings must be further refined, however, to link specific maternal personality disorders with specific child disturbances. In the same vein, depressed mother functioning between episodes should be examined in relation to specific personality disorders.

Age at Onset of Depression

The age of the individual at the onset of major affective disorders has been interpreted as a sign of genetic risk. A number of studies (e.g., Weissman, Wickramaratne, Merikangas, Leckman, Prusoff, Caruso, Kidd, & Gammon, 1984; Orvaschel et al., 1988) provide evidence linking early onset of depressive illness in adult probands with higher rates of depression in their relatives, including their children.

Family Histories of Psychiatric Disorders

There are findings relating higher rates of depression in offspring to affective and other psychiatric problems among relatives of depressed probands (Weissman, Kidd, & Prusoff, 1982; Weissman, Gershon, Kidd, Prusoff, Leckman, Dibble, Hamovit, Thompson, Pauls, & Guroff, 1984). There are higher rates of bipolar I and major depression in relatives of bipolar patients, and higher rates of major depression in relatives of major depression patients.

Overall, many facets of mothers' diagnosis and illness history have been found to affect the rates of offspring problems. It remains for research to determine their cumulative or interactive influences on offspring outcomes.

HOW DOES THE FAMILY ENVIRONMENT INFLUENCE OFFSPRING DEVELOPMENT?

Research has focused on stress in the family as a mediator of the transmission of psychopathology to the offspring. The frequent presence of discord and disorganization in families with a depressed parent is well known (Brown & Harris, 1978). This finding has led to numerous investigations posing the question of relative importance of parental diagnosis and family stress. The mode of research has been to classify families in broad categories of stressful events and conditions, based on interviews or questionnaires; then, through statistical controls, to attempt to evaluate the separate contributions to children's problems of various stressors. Findings have varied, and investigators have come to differing conclusions, as illustrated by three studies that are representative of the methods of research and the unsettled state of results on this question: the Stony Brook study (Emery et al., 1982), the study by Hammen, Gordon, Burge, Adrian, Jaenicke, and Hiroto (1987), and a report from the Yale longitudinal study (Fendrich, Warner, & Weissman, 1990).

Emery et al. examined marital disharmony in relation to the school performance of children of affectively ill and normal control parents. These authors conclude that, once marital discord is taken into account (statistically controlled), there are no significant associations between parental depression and children's school performance.

Hammen et al. report contrary findings, but with different measures. Child assessments include psychiatric diagnoses as well as mothers' CBCL reports and teachers' ratings. As in the Stony Brook study, the goal was to evaluate the contributions of maternal depression and chronic strains in family life to child outcomes.

The authors conclude that ongoing strain in the family contributes to child outcomes beyond the influences of maternal illness alone.

Fendrich et al. examined family environment in terms of marital discord, divorce, "affectionless control," and family cohesion. Brief questionnaires were used. Consistent with other research, they found more stressful family conditions in families of depressed than in families of nondepressed parents. In the offspring of depressed parents, only conduct disorder was associated with low family cohesiveness and parent–child discord. With nondepressed parents, significant associations were found between many of the family stress variables and children's problems. The authors conclude that family "risk factors are more adverse for children of nondepressed parents than for children of depressed parents." They further conclude that parental depression has a "direct influence" on offspring problems and that family risk factors contribute little more. These interpretations have been challenged by Rutter (1990): (1) Because the risk for depression in the Fendrich et al. study is not significantly different for the offspring of depressed and nondepressed parents, there is no support for the conclusion of direct effects of diagnosis on child pathology. (2) Family stress conditions in the control families are infrequent, whereas high proportions of the ill families have stress conditions – thereby complicating analyses and interpretations across groups.

If these studies are a reasonable sample of research on family influences, we see that there is a vast area of unknowns regarding processes. The many studies of family stress and offspring problems, with the repetition of variable findings, raise concerns regarding the adequacy of the research questions and the methods of study. More studies of similar design probably will not advance an understanding of maternal diagnosis and stress as joint influences on offspring. This area of research cannot simply be set aside, however. The centrality of this issue for understanding offspring problems emphasizes the need for appraisal of the approaches that have been taken.

A number of shortcomings, in our opinion, contribute to the

unstable findings. First is the lack of specificity in assessing the family environment. The broadly defined areas of stress (e.g., marital discord, losses, etc.) cover very diverse conditions across families, and are likely to impact uniquely on individual family members. Individual differences in children's responses to stress need attention. The research on successful or resilient offspring, despite high-risk family conditions, has documented the importance of qualities of the child (e.g., intellectual, temperamental) in responses to stress (e.g., Garmezy, 1985; Rutter, 1985; Masten, Garmezy, Tellegen, Pelligrini, Larkin, & Larsen, 1988; Radke-Yarrow & Sherman, 1990; Luthar, 1991; Radke-Yarrow & Brown, 1992).

Further, the contexts in which a given family stressor occurs have been ignored. A personal loss, for example, may occur amid other turbulent family conditions, or its effects may be muted by the presence of protective factors. A clear example of the importance of context is the finding cited by Werner and Smith (1982). In their study of high- and low-risk families in Kauai, good parenting was unrelated to child outcome in the low-risk families, but highly related to child outcomes in the high-risk families.

A further major limitation in the assessment of family environment derives from the fact that family functioning and depressed parent–child relationships have been investigated separately, although, quite clearly, they are interrelated sources of stress. Difficulties in mothering by depressed women constitute stressors for the children. Very possibly these stressors have origins in other family relationships, and also contribute to other relationships. Therefore, parenting variables and family variables need to be brought together in research.

Depressed mothers have been faulted on many dimensions of mothering. Impaired child management and disciplinary practices have been found in depressed mothers (Davenport, Zahn-Waxler, Adland, & Mayfield, 1984, bipolar mothers; Forehand, Lautenschlager, Faust, & Graziano, 1986; Cox, et al., 1987; Kochanska, Kuczynski, Radke-Yarrow, & Welsh, 1987). Negative attitudes toward parenting and perceptions of self as incompetent are characteristics reported by Weissman and Paykel (1974) and Webster-Stratton and Hammond (1988). Depressed mothers were found to be more irritable and hostile than control mothers by Hammen et al. (1987a). Sadness and anxiety were expressed more often by depressed mothers in interactions with their children (Hops, Biglan, Sherman, Arthur, Friedman, & Osteen, 1987; Radke-Yarrow, Nottelmann, Belmont, & Welsh, 1993). Inattention, lack of sensitivity to child's cues, and psychological unavailability are cited as characteristic of depressed mothers by Cox et al. (1987) and Goodman and Brumley (1990). Negative appraisals of their children were more likely from depressed mothers (Forehand et al., 1986). Lack of communicative synchrony and pleasure in depressed mother–child interaction were reported by Grunebaum, Cohler, Kaufman, and Gallant (1978). One by one, these difficulties in affect regulation, communication, self-absorption, and intimate relationships give depressed parenting the profile of depression.

Because we have had two separate literatures – depressed mothers' behavior and stress areas in family functioning – we have little knowledge concerning their cumulative or interacting influences on the children.

WHAT ARE THE EXPLANATIONS FOR CROSS-GENERATIONAL TRANSMISSION OF PSYCHOPATHOLOGY?

This question remains the persistent question. The overarching theoretical model of interacting genetic and environmental factors is not specific on the transmission of depression; it gives only general direction to research.

The many pieces of evidence at the level of associations have not been integrated. Because they are based mainly on cross-sectional studies, the associations require cautious, causal interpretation. Because age of offspring and timing of disorders have received rather casual treatment, the significance of development as a variable to aid in identifying transmission processes has not been extensively investigated.

A grand theory, at this time in research knowledge, does not

23

seem a realistic objective. The work ahead for research is to deal with the complexities of transmission. Research questions and approaches need to take account of multiple factors as interactive in their influences on offspring outcomes.

4

RESEARCH DESIGN AND PROCEDURES

The study takes place in the context of the nuclear family in urban United States, and reflects the perspectives on development and psychopathology that are characteristic of this milieu. Families were chosen for the study who present differences in risk to their children because of differences in parents' psychiatric status – affective illness or wellness.

RECRUITMENT AND SELECTION

Multiple criteria entered into the selection of families. A main criterion was the mother's diagnosis of unipolar depression, bipolar illness, or absence of any psychiatric diagnosis. Other primary diagnoses were ruled out to allow us to focus solely on the characteristics and consequences of maternal depression and its correlates. The fathers' status was also limited to wellness, depression, or anxiety.

The composition of the family further determined eligibility for the study. Families were selected in which father, mother, a child of 1½ to 3½ years of age and a second child of 5 to 8 years of age were present. In all families, the mother was the primary caregiver for both children; their experience together had been without long or frequent separations. These criteria brought parents into the study who were relatively young, and who, by virtue of the ages of the children, were at similar stages of family history and were dealing with similar family tasks. Control of the children's ages allowed us to have a clear developmental context in evaluating children's functioning.

Our participants are community-dwelling families who volunteered to be studied (later screened in detail). Our focus is not on population-representativeness, or on establishing representative rates of children's psychopathology, but on relations among variables that are relevant to children's development, and to parent-to-child transmission processes. Selection criteria were specifically in the service of these research objectives.

The families in this study would be expected to differ in a number of ways from a population-representative sample of depressed parents and also from a hospitalized or clinic-referred parent sample. Treatment samples may be more severely depressed, and may have heavier loading of pathology in their family histories than community-based samples. However, differences between hospitalized and community-living patients are likely to have changed over the years. Many seriously affectively ill individuals, who are now being treated with antidepressants and lithium and are living in the community, would probably have been hospitalized in earlier studies. Factors that enter into treatment decisions are not well known.

Parents who are hospitalized for long periods of time cannot be the primary child-rearing agents. A basic consideration was to have affectively ill parents performing in the parental role. The criterion of family intactness at the time of entrance into the study also makes our families nonrepresentative of depressed families in the population, for whom rates of separation and divorce are high (Fendrich et al., 1990). Also, our well families were more than a "not ill" group, at the time of selection. These families were intact, without severe marital problems, and without major physical health problems.

The families were recruited through repeated announcements in newspapers, to parent groups, and to clinicians. The first announcement read as follows:

MOTHERS
* an important message*
The National Institute of Mental Health (NIMH)
Laboratory of Developmental Psychology
is looking for women to participate

26

in a study about childrearing and
emotional development

We are particularly interested in hearing from mothers who have experienced feelings of depression or mood swings, and mothers who may have sought help or taken medications for these problems.

To be eligible,
you must have at least **two children**.
One must be 1½ to 3½ years old.
A second must be **5** to **8** years old.

Mothers will be **paid** for their participation according to the guidelines of the NIH Normal Volunteer Program.

Notices provided a telephone number. Approximately 500 calls were received in the first recruitment efforts. Telephone interviews were the first level of detailed screening. If the family passed this screening, the mothers were asked to come to the laboratory for a structured psychiatric interview (Schedule for Affective Disorders and Schizophrenia, SADS-L, Spitzer & Endicott, 1977; RDC criteria, Spitzer, Endicott & Robins, 1978). Interviews were conducted by a psychiatric nurse, trained by a staff member of the New York Psychiatric Institute. Ten interviews were coded independently by nurse and trainer with 100% agreement on diagnosis.

If the mother met criteria, the father was given a SADS-L interview. Spouses of affectively ill mothers were without a psychiatric disorder, or met criteria for depression or anxiety, without other problems. Spouses of well mothers had to be without past or current psychiatric disorders. Recruitment took place over a 2½-year period.

Six years into the study, parents were again given a psychiatric assessment, a lifetime SCID (Structured Clinical Interview for DSM-III-R; Spitzer, Williams, Gibbon, & First, 1989). To accord with earlier assessments, an interval SADS was also administered. The clinicians administering the interview had no prior contact with the families and were blind to earlier diagnoses.

27

To arrive at a mother's lifetime diagnosis, the psychiatric interview assessments at the time of admission to the study and at the follow-up were taken into account. Differences in these assessments occurred in nine cases. Two well mothers and three mothers with minor depression (a diagnosis originally included, but dropped), had developed major depression, and four mothers with depression had developed bipolar illness. Attrition from the original sample at the third assessment period was 12.7%. Four families with well mothers and four with major or bipolar depression refused. In one family, both parents had died. The other families could not be located.

LONGITUDINAL STUDY GROUP

The study group on which this longitudinal report is based is 98 families in which the mother's lifetime diagnosis is major (unipolar) depression ($n = 42$), bipolar illness ($n = 26$), or well ($n = 30$). These are families who have remained with the study through successive stages of assessment and whose psychiatric assessment meets criteria (Table 4.1).

Changes in diagnoses over time occurred in six of the fathers, but these changes did not alter the family classification. Changes were to depression, anxiety, or substance abuse. Fathers for whom a second diagnostic interview was not done were given their initial diagnosis unless some clear evidence indicated otherwise (e.g., father is in treatment for substance abuse). (At the first assessment, 95% of the fathers were evaluated; at the second assessment, 74% were evaluated.) At the time of the final assessment, 65% and 64% of the husbands in the families with bipolar and unipolar mothers, respectively, had a psychiatric disorder.

The demographic characteristics of the families are as follows: 87% of well families, 89% of families of bipolar mothers, and 83% of families of unipolar mothers are Caucasian-American; 10%, 8%, and 14% are African-American; and 3%, 4%, and 0% are Hispanic-American. In the order of well, bipolar, and unipolar groups, the educational level of the mothers is college graduate or more in

28

Table 4.1 *The study group* (n = 98)

	Mother's diagnosis					
	Well (*n* = 30)		Bipolar (*n* = 26)		Unipolar (*n* = 42)	
Mother's age *M* (*SD*) at Time 1	32.6	(4.5)	32.4	(3.5)	32.7	(4.9)
Father's age *M* (*SD*) at Time 1	34.6	(4.2)	35.9	(6.1)	35.6	(4.5)
Younger siblings						
Number of boys	16		12		21	
Number of girls	14		14		21	
M (*SD*) age						
Time 1	2.6	(0.6)	2.9	(0.6)	2.5	(0.6)
Time 2	5.5	(0.5)	5.6	(0.6)	5.6	(0.6)
Time 3	9.5	(1.1)	9.0	(1.0)	9.3	(1.1)
Time 4	13.8	(1.9)	13.3	(1.5)	14.2	(1.6)
M (*SD*) IQ	120	(15.1)	113	(18.2)	116	(17.0)
Older siblings						
Number of boys	14		7		18	
Number of girls	16		15		24	
M (*SD*) age						
Time 1	6.2	(0.8)	6.5	(1.3)	6.5	(1.0)
Time 2	9.0	(1.1)	9.2	(1.4)	9.6	(1.2)
Time 3	13.0	(1.5)	13.0	(1.7)	13.3	(1.3)
Time 4	17.3	(2.2)	17.1	(1.9)	18.2	(1.7)
M (*SD*) IQ	122	(12.1)	112	(15.0)	116	(16.3)

Note: Four of the families with a bipolar mother have only one child, in the cohort of younger children.

81%, 62%, and 56%; some college, 18%, 25%, 27%; high school, 0%, 13%, and 15%. One mother was not a high school graduate. A number of mothers were continuing their education during the years of the study. The means and standard deviations on Hollingshead ratings of socioeconomic level for well, bipolar, and unipolar families, respectively, at the beginning of the study, were 56.4 (10.6), 50.5 (14.3), and 47.7 (16.0). At the beginning of the study, 95% of the families were intact. In the course of the study, separations or divorces occurred in 26% of the families of unipolar mothers, in 35% of the families of bipolar mothers, and in 13% of the families of well mothers.

Further Illness Characteristics of the Mothers

Diagnostic characteristics of the families were further specified for analytic purposes. The mother's illness history, course, and functional impairment and her personality disorders were determined. As estimates of the degree of functional impairment, the Global Assessment Scales (GAS, Endicott, Spitzer, Fleiss, & Cohen, 1976) and the Global Assessment of Functioning (GAF, a revision of GAS, Diagnostic and Statistical Manual of Mental Disorders, 1987) were used at initial and follow-up diagnoses.

Several years into the study, the mother and father were interviewed about mental illness in their first and second degree relatives (Family History-Research Diagnostic Criteria, Endicott, Andreasen, & Spitzer, 1975). These data have limitations, resting on the recall and interpretations of the informants. Mental illness information on a relative was classified as an affective disorder (unipolar or bipolar), a mental problem, or an addiction problem.

The Personality Disorder Examination (PDE; Loranger, 1988) was administered to the mother at the time of the second diagnostic interview (SCID). The PDE is a semistructured clinical interview that assesses symptomatology according to the DSM-III-R classification system (Axis II). Personality characteristics are assumed to be "enduring patterns of perceiving, relating to, and thinking about the environment and oneself." For a disorder to be scored, it has been present for at least five years. Disorders are classified as: Cluster A = paranoid, schizoid, schizotypal; Cluster B = antisocial, borderline, histrionic, narcissistic, sadistic; Cluster C = avoidant, dependent, obsessive, passive aggressive, self-defeating. We scored the PDE categorically (mother has or has not a given disorder) and also dimensionally (the sum of symptoms). Intraclass correlations from independent scoring of individual dimensional scores averaged .90 (see DeMulder, Tarullo, Klimes-Dougan, Free, & Radke-Yarrow, 1995, for a full report).

Table 4.2 *Schedule of assessments, by ages of children and sibling cohort*

	Ages of children				
	1½ to 3½ years	5 to 7 years	8 to 11 years	11 to 15 years	15 to 19 years
Younger siblings	T1	T2	T3	T4	
Older siblings		T1	T2	T3	T4

THE STUDY DESIGN

A longitudinal design makes it possible to observe stabilities and changes in the organization of behavior and in the conditions associated with development. The identity of the individual child and the family is preserved, and, increasingly, one learns much about the families, beyond the data from the standard procedures.

Like most longitudinal studies, this study is a follow-up design with intensive assessments at spaced intervals (see Table 4.2). The times of evaluations are important in determining how development is "captured." Assessments were timed to coincide with transitional developmental periods.

Assessment Periods

At initial assessment (T1), the younger siblings, between 1½ and 3½ years (mean = 2.63, SD = 0.6), were leaving toddlerhood and were dealing with developmental tasks of autonomy strivings, socialization demands, and developing relationships. In this period, the family is the predominant context. The older siblings, at initial assessment, between 5 and 8 years (mean = 6.39, SD = 1.0), represented a developmental transition to early school age. In normative expectations, they would have developed increased self-control and self-identity. The added demands and opportunities of peers and school would have expanded their social relationships.

At the second assessment period (T2), the younger siblings had reached the school-age transition period (between 5 and 6 years, mean = 5.54, SD = 0.5). The older siblings were in middle to late childhood (8 to 11 years, mean = 9.31, SD = 1.2). In normal development, children would have consolidated earlier developmental accomplishments, would have the benefits of far more complex cognitive abilities, and would have expanded independence.

At the third assessment (T3), the younger children were in middle to late childhood (mean = 9.26, SD = 1.1); the older siblings were approaching or were in adolescence (11 to 15 years, mean = 13.06, SD = 1.5). In addition to pubertal changes, child–parent relationships and peer influences in this period are also changing, and extrafamilial demands are assuming ever greater prominence. Special demands on the parental role are likely to increase as adolescent complexities and conflicts increase.

At the fourth assessment (T4), many of the younger siblings had moved into adolescence (mean = 13.88, SD = 1.7) and the older siblings were in middle to late adolescence or early adulthood (15 to 19 years, mean = 17.5, SD = 2.0). Normatively, relationships with parents would be renegotiated in this period, and the young person would be becoming absorbed in his/her own life course.

Because the age spacing of the two siblings coincides roughly with the time spacing between assessments, data on the two children provide an approximate age replication within the study. In addition, observing the development of two siblings provides the opportunity to examine the uniquenesses and similarities in psychosocial development in the same family.

Principles of Assessment

The selection of procedures was guided by three major considerations: (1) Child assessments should cover a broad spectrum of theoretically relevant aspects of functioning. (2) The behavioral environment should be conceptualized and measured at levels of specificity similar to levels used in measuring person variables. Environmental measures should be based on theory-justified sampling of behavior. (3) Multiple sources of information should be utilized.

PROCEDURES

Observations of behavior, interviews, and tests are the sources of data. Child assessments include affective–cognitive, regulatory, and relationship dimensions. Environmental assessments tap parental and family behavior that is assumed to be facilitating or interfering with child behavior, and that is most likely to be affected by maternal depression.

A first objective was to establish a comfortable research setting and a trusting relationship that could endure over a long period of time. The laboratory setting was an apartment in a spacious old house in the midst of a campus of large institutional buildings. The apartment was a suite of rooms with adjoining kitchen cove and bathroom (Fig. 4.1). The families came for many visits over the years. Usually the visits were half-days or longer in duration. The setting became familiar and comfortable. One staff member served throughout the study as the liaison person responsible for a continuing relationship with the families. She came to know the families well, and they came to know and trust her.

Observed Behavior

Observation of behavior is a major procedure, especially for early and middle childhood. It provides information on the patterned behavior of each family member, the environment that mother and child make for each other, and, to a lesser extent, the environment of father with child, and sibling with sibling.

In the first period of assessment (T1), the mother came to the apartment with her toddler on given days; other days with both the toddler and the early school-age child. The schedule of events in the long periods of time in the apartment was planned to be

Figure 4.1. Research apartment.

as natural as possible without sacrificing the control needed for measurement purposes. Time was planned to mimic the range and variety of ordinary, expected, day-to-day experiences, and to sample situations that tap critical aspects of child rearing at different developmental stages, and aspects most likely to be affected by mother's illness.

Mother and child found themselves in usual routines (e.g., preparing a meal, eating lunch, cleaning up), facing ambiguities of new experiences, frustrations, dealing with burdening multiple demands, and separations. There were activities and interactions that were savored and relaxing, as well as encounters that were somewhat stressful. We encouraged the families to make the apartment "their own," which included helping themselves to contents of cupboard and refrigerator and using telephone, TV, and play materials. We introduced standard, structured paradigms into these sequences, for example the Strange Situation to measure the attachment relationship (Ainsworth, Blehar, Waters, & Wall, 1978), a "doctor's" anthropometric examination as a standard potential stressor, and a modified behavioral inhibition paradigm (Kagan, Resnick, Clark, Snidman, & Garcia-Coll, 1984).

The second assessment period (T2), three years later, again utilized similar events and conditions. The father was present on one of the days. Age changes in the children dictated some change in activities, although situations were conceptually similar – presenting challenge, enjoyment, uncertainty, stress, and accomplishment.

In the third assessment period (T3), the family came for a full day. Since the two children were now in middle childhood and adolescence, the naturalness of events was less feasible. However, tasks were kept "real," staying close to everyday experience or problems, (e.g., meal together, mother and each child being asked to discuss their relationship with each other). The fourth evaluation (T4) was confined to psychiatric and psychological interviews.

The laboratory rooms are equipped for audio–visual recording. The families were informed of the recording and were invited to inspect the viewing room. Their behavior was coded from videotape. Units of behavior and coding categories varied from macro to micro. Coders were blind to all assessments of the parents and children. However, maternal behavior, in many instances, provided coders with information about the mother's illness.

Mother's Behavior in Macro Coding. The mother's behavior in the apartment, with each of her children, was evaluated in domains of affect, communication, and control, using ratings. There were approximately six total hours of videotaped interaction with the younger sibling and three hours with the older sibling at assessment Times 1 and 2.

The mother's behavior was observed in time blocks of approximately an hour, which coincided with natural breaks in the scripted half-day sessions. The coder rated the mother's actions and words for involvement and interest in the child, demonstration of positive and negative feelings and attitudes toward the child, support and encouragement of the child, efforts to set limits or standards, and expressed affect (enjoyment and pleasure, irritability and anger, warmth and tenderness).

The coder observed each period of interaction as many times as she wished before rating maternal behavior (0 to 5) on how little or how much a given behavior was characteristic of the mother. For example, how characteristic is: "Mother is facilitating, supporting, encouraging child?" (M ICC = .61 based on 24 cases, range .38 to .74) (Bartko, Strauss, & Carpenter, 1980). The periods in which standard paradigms were introduced (such as the Strange Situation) were not included in these observations. The fathers' behavior was coded similarly but on a more limited behavior sample (2 hours) at T2.

At T3, the mother's behavior was similarly coded (M ICC = .62) in a standard setting with each child, separately. Mother and child were asked to discuss their relationship with one another. They were given sample questions to begin their discussion (e.g., "How do you think you and I are alike and different?" "I like some things about being a mother and some things I don't like. What do you think they are?"). This 10-minute, somewhat stressful, interaction came at the end of a day of psychiatric evaluations and situations involving family interaction (see Tarullo, DeMulder, Martinez, & Radke-Yarrow, 1994, for full account).

36

Mother's Behavior in Micro Coding. Finer-grained coding was used for aspects of mother's relationships with her children:

(1) For each instance in which the mother made an attempt to regulate the toddler's behavior (T1), we coded her methods of regulating the child's behavior (kappas = .67 to .91, based on 26 situations) and her successes and failures in child management (kappas = .85 to .90, based on 26 situations) (see Kochanska et al. 1987).

(2) The behavior of mother and child in the Strange Situation was coded for the security/insecurity of the *attachment* relationship (67% to 80% agreement before conferencing) (see DeMulder & Radke-Yarrow, 1991).

(3) A clinician, blind to the psychiatric assessments of mother and child, evaluated each mother on signs of overinvestment in the child – for overly *dependent and engulfing* behavior with her child (kappa = .86, based on 17 cases).

(4) The mother's *expressed moods and emotions* were observed. Each minute in the apartment (excluding the standard paradigms) was rated for predominant affect – for expression of sad, anxious–fearful, irritable–angry, downcast–somber, pleasant–joyful, and tender–affectionate affect (ICCs from .85 to .98) (see Radke-Yarrow, Nottelmann, Belmont, & Welsh, 1993).

Children's Behavior. The child's behavior in the apartment was observed alone and in interactions with the mother (as indicated above). The rating systems used to macro and micro code parent behavior were used for parallel child behavior. The coder focused on the child's behavior regulation, affective expression and regulation, and relationship with the mother (ICCs from .52 to .98). Interactions with the father and the sibling were similarly coded (ICCs from .49 to .82, M = .66).

The Strange Situation (Ainsworth et al., 1978) assessment of the *attachment relationship*, was coded following the manual for preschool age children (Cassidy, Marvin, & MacArthur Working Group on Attachment, 1987/89). Attachment was assessed only for the younger siblings.

Assessment of *behavioral inhibition* followed a modified version of the Novel Situation (Kagan et al., 1984) (see Kochanska, 1991). The child's ability to approach and explore the physical and social environment was coded (kappas = .84 and .89).

Interviews and Inventories

Interviews and inventories are the second major source of data. Structured interviews provide psychiatric evaluations of the parents, as already described. The children were interviewed at each age, except in the preschool ages. Measures of children's functioning in school and with peers, their self-regard, their processing of their mother's illness and parental behavior are children's self-assessments and mother and teacher reports. Interviews with the mother provide data on family functioning.

Child Psychiatric Assessments. For *children under four years of age,* the psychiatrist's "interview" was a *play session* consisting of a standard sequence of situations designed to challenge the child in various ways: namely, the child's ability to separate from the mother, relate to an unfamiliar adult, explore the environment, and express and manage affect appropriately. The psychiatrist talked briefly with the mother and child before inviting the child to come in to play. The child's separation from the mother was evaluated. If the child could not tolerate separation from the mother, the door was left open, and/or the child was given the opportunity to make contact with the mother.

The session has three 10- to 12-minute segments. In the first segment, the child is invited to play with a standard set of relatively neutral toys (blocks, crayons and paper, ball, doll, teddy bear). After 10 minutes, the psychiatrist asks the child to help put away the toys and bring out new toys. In the second segment, a doll house and dolls matched to the child's family provide possibilities for play relevant to the child's family. The psychiatrist helps to involve the child by identifying "mother," "sister," and so on, but is nondirective. After 10 minutes, a change is made to toys that have high potential for aggressive play (guns, soldiers, punching bag, boxing gloves, pounding blocks).

The psychiatrist evaluated the child on (1) separation anxiety, (2) generalized anxiety, (3) disruptive or oppositional behavior, and (4) depressed affect. Taking into consideration the age of the child, the psychiatrist made a judgment as to whether the child was exhibiting behavior judged to be of clinical concern: (1) whether the behavior was sufficiently deviant to suggest the need for treatment and/or close monitoring and (2) whether the behavior posed a serious risk to, or interference with, the normal course of development. Ten cases were scored from videotapes by a second psychiatrist with agreement ranging from 86% to 98% on specific problem areas. The overall kappa is .82. Both psychiatrists were blind to parent diagnoses, as far as this is possible, because the mother's behavior provides clues.

In making a final psychiatric assessment of the preschool age child, the mother's report of child problems on the Child Behavior Check List (CBCL; Achenbach & Edelbrock, 1979, 1983) was used in combination with the psychiatrist's evaluation of the play session. At the time the study began, there was no CBCL scale for anxiety and no scale for preschool-age children. Therefore, mothers' reports only with regard to disruptive/oppositional behavior (delinquency and aggression scales) were considered. The mother's perspective was added because it was assumed that disruptive/oppositional behavior might be underestimated by the psychiatrist who saw the child only in the play session. Based on norms for 6- to 11-year-olds, a child with a T score at or above the 90th percentile was considered of clinical concern. This assessment was combined with the psychiatrist's evaluation.

For *children 5 years of age and older* (T1 & T2), a semistructured psychiatric interview, the Child Assessment Schedule (CAS; Hodges, Kline, Fitch, McKnew, & Cytryn, 1981), was used. The interview was designed to assess children's fears, moods, somatic concerns, anger, self-image, and thought disorders. Interviewers (either a psychiatrist or psychologist) were blind to the diagnostic status of parents and sibling and prior assessments of the child. The interviews were analyzed from video and/or audio record by two child psychiatrists who had no knowledge of the psychiatric status of parents or sibling.

39

Problem areas of anxiety, depression, and disruptive behavior were scored according to DSM-III-R classifications. Final assessment at this age was again a combination of the CAS and the mother's CBCL reports, using normed T scores at or above the 90th percentile on narrow-band scales of depressive behavior, delinquent behavior, and aggressive behavior. For reliability estimates, both psychiatrists coded 25 cases. Agreement on assignment of problems of disruptive, anxious, and depressive problems is a kappa of .83.

It is well known that psychiatric assessment of preschool and early school-age children presents nosological and procedural difficulties. There are no clearly established criteria for what constitutes a "problem" on a given dimension at a given young age, yet the use of categorical diagnoses forces a cut-point. In this study, a "diagnosis" at the younger ages is regarded as a warning level of deviance from (our best judgment of) the age "norm."

Each instrument used here has strengths and weaknesses. Assessment from the play interview rests on real behavior, but it is difficult to calibrate finely. Limited language abilities of the child put constraints on the structured interview and necessitate great sensitivity in interpreting children's understanding and responses. Behavioral cues are of valuable assistance. Mothers' reports furnish the second perspective. Mothers are, of necessity, the sole source of information regarding some critical aspects of the child's functioning.

At *Time 3*, the Diagnostic Interview for Children and Adolescents (DICA; Herjanic & Reich, 1982) was used for assessment of the child's functioning since the last assessment and at the present time. Child (DICA) and mother (DICA-P) were interviewed. The same interviewer conducted both interviews, as would be done in a clinical setting. The interviewers were trained and supervised by a child psychiatrist. Interviewers were blind to all other information on the children and their families. Percent agreement on the designation of individual problem areas, based on 26 children, ranged from 79% to 100%. The overall kappa, based on coding of the videotaped interviews of 63 younger and 76 older siblings, is

.82 for younger children and .84 for older children. The DICA was scored for the full range of DSM-III-R diagnoses. Symptom counts in specific problem areas were also made.

At *Time 4*, the children were given an abbreviated DICA, covering the sections on affective disorders, and the Symptom Checklist (SCL 90-R; Derogatis, 1983).

The mother's CBCL report was obtained at all assessment periods. In middle childhood, a CBCL report was obtained from teachers. This proved very difficult to obtain because it involved so many school systems. The CBCL was analyzed in terms of total problem scores, internalizing and externalizing scores, and on narrow band scales. A cut-point for a clinical problem is the 90th percentile.

At Time 4, information was also obtained from the parent and child regarding *critical developments* involving the child, such as hospitalizations, drugs, pregnancies, trouble with the law, college and career progress.

Age as a Classificatory Criterion. Developmental studies face a serious problem in making successive evaluations of groups of children, when using age as the criterion of "sameness" across children. Through the childhood years, age seems a reasonable criterion. Chronological age in the childhood years classifies children into relatively homogeneous maturational groups (T1, T2, T3 for the younger siblings and T1, T2 for the older siblings). We have designated ages up to 11 as the prepubertal years, although a few children have reached puberty.

Around age 11, differences in pubertal development for children of the same chronological age introduce biological and social role heterogeneity. We have represented time from 11 to 15 years as late childhood to early adolescence, and 15 to 19 as adolescence.

Children's Social Functioning. Information on children's relationships with peers and their functioning in school was based on combined data from child, parent, and teacher. At T3, children reported their satisfactions and dissatisfactions with family mem-

41

bers and friends using a semistructured interview, "My Family and Friends" (Reid, Landesman, Treder, & Jaccard, 1989).

Cognitive Measures. At T3, the Harter Scale of Perceived Competence (Harter, 1979) provided a measure of the child's self-concept. Also at this time each child was given the Wechsler Intelligence Scale for Children (WISC-R; Wechsler, 1974).

Assessment of Family Functioning. Behavior observed in the laboratory is a small sample of individual dispositions and relationships, and cannot convey the chronicity and fluctuations in interpersonal experiences or note the critical or crisis events in the family. For information on family conditions and functioning in the larger life setting, mothers were interviewed. In a Brown–Harris (1978) schedule for assessing family functioning, modified by Pellegrini (1982), areas of marital relationships, conflicts and problems between and among other family members, health problems, losses of significant persons, and problems of housing, job, and economics were explored. Mothers' first interview was just prior to or at T2. Mothers were asked to recall events and conditions that existed prior to and at the time the family entered the study, and also to describe current conditions. The timing of events and conditions was reported. Mothers were interviewed again just preceding T3 assessment.

The recorded interview responses were first organized by "blind" editors who brought together all material relating to each content area. Each area was then rated on seriousness of stress (ratings 0 to 4) (kappas range from .61 to .97).

Further information on family functioning came from the children's reflections on their growing-up experiences, and from a longitudinal log record.

Physical Status

At T3, each child was given a pediatric examination. Pubertal status (Tanner staging) was included in the examination, although it was an assessment that children often refused.

Longitudinal Log

From the beginning of the study, a log was maintained to preserve information relating to the family. Sources are: (1) notes on visits to the participants' home and telephone calls to and from the participants, (2) comments and behavior of participants when at the laboratory, and (3) clinicians' write-ups following diagnostic procedures and feedback sessions with parents. In the feedback sessions, the clinician provided parents with information about their children and dealt with needed interventions. The parents often furnished information about events and conditions between periods of assessment (e.g., child had been hospitalized, grandparent committed suicide, child was placed in a special school for talented children). Often significant developments in the parents' and children's lives came to light. Without the log, the intimate "running account" of the lives of these families would have been lost.

Clinical Responsibilities

For mothers who had a diagnosis and who became participants in the study, it was required (or arranged) that they have available a mental health professional. After each series of assessments, the psychiatrist met with the parents to discuss the information that had been gathered. Where intervention seemed necessary, he helped the parents in obtaining professional assistance and, in emergencies, directly arranged help. The families were also free to call the psychiatrist or liaison person at times between assessments.

OVERVIEW OF ANALYSES

The procedures used to assess parents and children at each time period are listed in Tables 4.3 and 4.4. Multimethods, multisources, and multicontextual sources make different levels of analysis possible. In the following chapters, we search for relations between and among variables of parental diagnosis, behavioral environment, properties of the child and maladaptive and adaptive

Table 4.3 *Study procedures: Assessments of parents and family*

Procedures	Time of assessment
Assessment of mother	
SADS-L[a]	T1
SCID[b] and Interval SADS	T3
PDE[c]	T3
POMS[d]	T1, T2
Observations in apartment with each child	T1, T2, T3
Observations in apartment with family	T1, T2, T3
Family history interview	T2
Assessment of father	
SADS-L	T1
SCID and Interval SADS	T3
Observations in apartment with each child	T2, T3
Observations in apartment with family	T2, T3
Family history interview	T2
Assessment of family functioning	
Life events and conditions interview with mother	T2, T3
Observations in apartment with family	T2, T3

[a]SADS-L: Schedule for Affective Disorders and Schizophrenia - Lifetime.
[b]SCID: Structured Clinical Interview for DSM-III-R.
[c]PDE: Personality Disorder Examination.
[d]POMS: Profile of Moods.

child "outcomes." In the majority of analyses, the outcome variable is categorical. Independent variables are categorical, ordinal, or continuous. Our continuous variables rarely meet the necessary assumptions of normality and are, therefore, most often rank ordered or categorized prior to being entered into analyses. Most often, both independent and dependent variables are categorical. The most frequently used data analysis techniques are, therefore, categorical:

1. Pearson's Chi-square or Fisher's Exact Test for homogeneity or independence is used when a single independent variable is of interest.

Table 4.4 *Study procedures: Assessment of children*

Procedures	Sibling group	Time of assessment
Psychiatric play interview	Younger	T1
CAS[a]	Older	T1, T2
CAS	Younger	T2
DICA[b]	Both	T3
DICA-P[c]	Both	T3
DICA (affective scales)	Both	T4
Symptom Checklist 90-R	Both	T4
CBCL[d] (mother)	Both	T1, T2, T3, T4
CBCL (teacher)	Older	T1
CBCL (teacher)	Younger	T2
WISC-R[e]	Both	T3
Perceived Competence Scale for Children (Harter)	Both	T3
My Family and Friends Interview	Both	T3
Attachment paradigm	Younger	T1
Behavioral inhibition paradigm	Younger	T1, T2
Observations in apartment	Both	T1, T2, T3
Interview: Family experiences	Both	T4

[a]CAS: Child Assessment Schedule.
[b]DICA: Diagnostic Interview for Children and Adolescents.
[c]DICA-P: Diagnostic Interview for Children and Adolescents, mother interview about child.
[d]CBCL: Child Behavior Checklist.
[e]WISC-R: Wechsler Intelligence Scale for Children, revised.

2. We are often interested in possible interaction effects of two independent variables, in relation to child outcome. An example is the interaction of type of maternal behavior and child temperament, in relation to child "outcome." For this purpose the Weighted Least Squares (WLS) approach to linear model building (Grizzle, Starmer, & Koch, 1969) is most useful. This method allows for specification of independent and dependent variables and for the incorporation of interaction terms, as well as contrasts

among values of the independent variables. Hence, it is an analysis of variance approach to categorical data. To control cell sizes, we use this approach to examine contributions of, at the most, two independent variables. (We have previously described our reasons for selecting this method; see Radke-Yarrow, Nottelmann, Martinez, Fox, & Belmont, 1992.) The SAS CATMOD procedure, version 6.08, is used for these analyses (SAS Institute, 1990). We have also used the WLS method of analyzing repeated measures. In this type of analysis, we have limited the number of independent variables (other than time) to one (Koch, Landis, Freeman, & Freeman, 1977).

3. We use survival analysis to look at the timing of initial acquisition of a problem in relation to mothers' diagnoses (Kalbfleisch & Prentice, 1980; Singer & Willett, 1991). The product limit method is used to compute the survival functions, with log rank test to determine whether the curves might come from identical distributions. The SAS LIFETEST procedure is used for these analyses (SAS Institute, 1990).

4. We use Cochran–Mantel–Haenszel (CMH; Landis, Heyman, Koch, 1978) statistics to assess the effects of an independent variable in different groups or strata, such as boys and girls. This test grants a measure of statistical control when looking for effects that may apply to only one of the groups or strata. When the CMH Chi-square is significant, we examine the effect of the independent variable within each group.

5. Logistic regression is useful for selecting the best predictor or predictors of child outcome from a group of related variables. This is important, given that our independent variables are often highly interrelated, and one variable might be found to adequately explain the effects of several.

6. The kappa statistic is used for assessing interrater reliability for categorical measures (Bartko et al., 1980).

Other nonparametric methods used include:

1. Wilcoxon rank-sum test or Kruskal–Wallis test for similarity of distributions of ordinal data in different groups, such as stress levels for children with and without problem "outcome."

2. Kendall's tau-b for correlations of ordinal and continuous measures.

In instances of continuous outcome measures, we use the typical parametric statistics such as analysis of variance, regression analysis, Pearson correlations, and factor analysis. We use Intra-Class correlations for checking interrater reliability (Bartko et al., 1980).

Conceptual Considerations

What is learned about behavior depends, in part, on the units in which it is measured. A "snapshot" of the child or parent at a given moment or period of time can meaningfully focus on a behavior element, a broader domain of behavior, or a cohering pattern of varied behavioral properties. Behavior viewed as a process over time (e.g., the developmental sequence), too, can be examined in varied units. The behavior units in our analyses vary in all of these respects.

Part of discovery comes in discerning the differentiating sensitivities that these varied perspectives provide. In many assessments, we are dealing with single elements or domains of child behavior in relation to a single "independent" variable. In many analyses, we are examining configurations of variables, on the assumption that it is the patterning of factors, contemporaneously and over time, that is critical for the understanding of behavior (Cairns, 1986; Magnusson & Bergman, 1988; Rutter, 1988, 1989a).

Diverse mechanisms and behavioral outcomes are to be expected in offspring development. We have, therefore, not limited our attention to broad central tendencies, main effects, and the "average" offspring. In many respects, accounting for order in diversity is an uncharted course in analysis, in which the goal is to bring together the idiosyncrasies of individual behavior and the lawfulness of development.

5

CHILDREN OF DEPRESSED MOTHERS: CASE DESCRIPTIONS

[Children's] strengths and vulnerabilities, their manifestations of psychopathology, and their social environments constrain and influence each other in different
ways over time.

Coyne and Downey (1991, p. 408)

The natural histories of children of two affectively ill mothers,
described in the contexts of the family, illustrate these interacting
factors.

FAMILY J

Margaret and Michael were born to a mother with bipolar illness
and a father with major (but moderate) depression. The parents
were in their late 20s when the children were born. The pregnancies were planned and remembered as happy times by both parents. Margaret was one and a half years older than Michael.

Mrs. J grew up in an urban, middle-class family that provided
a supportive and caring environment that has continued to the
present. Mrs. J has a history of affective illness that began when
she was 18 years old, when she experienced her first episode of
mania. At least three episodes of major depression followed by
age 20. Her episodes of mania and depression have recurred frequently over the years.

Mr. J, too, had a stable family background. He had an episode

48

of depression at 18 years for which he was hospitalized. Since then he has experienced periods of depressed mood but never has he been incapacitated.

When Mrs. J became pregnant for the first time, she was hoping for a boy, but was not disappointed when Margaret was born. Margaret was an "easy baby." She slept well, was healthy, and adapted well to routines. Although Mrs. J stopped taking lithium during pregnancy, she did not decompensate and was able to care for Margaret without interruptions. When Michael was born, she was hoping for a girl so she would not have to buy new baby clothes, but was very happy with Michael. Both children had normal physical development during infancy and toddlerhood.

At the time of the family's first visit, Mrs. J volunteered long descriptions of her children. "Margaret was a *most* delightful baby, always so happy and content." She called her "my little doll to dress up." Mrs. J described Margaret as now having many characteristics similar to her own — strong-willed, stubborn, extremely talkative, and active. Michael, she said, was "sweet, kind and easy going — my favorite."

In the apartment, both children appeared distressed. Margaret (5 years) acted assertively and independently — but warily. Michael (3½ years) was very insecure and would not allow his mother out of his sight. When Mrs. J went into the bathroom, he called, "I love you."

Mrs. J was grumpy and impatient with both children and could not get them to cooperate with her. She vented her anger on Margaret, "You're nothing but trouble to me. I'll never bring you again." Margaret threw a violent tantrum, after which Michael declared to his mother that he was not going to be her boy friend any more.

Michael went to the next room and started punching the Bobo doll. He threw the clown to the floor and sat on top of it. Then he spied a toy broom and took it back to the other room where his mother was watching TV. He brandished the broom over his mother's head, crashing it down beside her on the sofa. Mrs. J responded, "Hey, Michael, who's your girl friend?" She lifted him to her lap. He put his arm around her neck and kissed her, but all the while hanging onto the broom. "I love you." "I love you, too."

When the family returned to the apartment the next day, the children were on good behavior. The "riot act" had been read to them, with undisclosed threats hanging over them.

Some months after these research visits, Mr. and Mrs. J separated. The children stayed with their mother and Mr. J visited them and took them out on a scheduled plan. Mrs. J's family frequently took care of the children when Mrs. J was most irritable or manic. They took charge during a period of her hospitalization.

In the three years between the first and second research assessment, life had not been easy for the children. Margaret was placed in therapy shortly after the family breakup. She was showing many symptoms of anxiety. She blamed herself for the family separation and she greatly missed her father. She was doing poorly in third grade and had no friends.

Michael was so anxious he worried when his mother went to the store. Would she come back? He demanded her help on things he could easily do by himself. He began taking money from his mother's purse. Then he bought her a present. In first grade, he was silly and oppositional.

Mother and children returned to the laboratory for the second research evaluation when Margaret was 8 and Michael was 6½. Michael demanded to leave. Mrs. J threatened to punish him if he didn't behave. Michael was loud, rude, and belligerent. Mrs. J tried to get him out of his bad mood by wrestling with him. To no avail.

Mrs. J told the children she wanted some peace and quiet for herself, wanted to watch a TV program. Mrs. J told them if they didn't stay out of her way, she'd lock them in the bathroom. The children retreated to the other room, reminding themselves of mother's threats. Finally they got into an argument. Mrs. J. yelled that she was going to put tape over Margaret's mouth. Margaret again got the blame at lunchtime. Her mother told her to stop talking and eat – hitting her for emphasis. Margaret finished quickly and went to the other room, leaving Michael and mother in friendly conversation.

Later both children were engaged in a puzzle task. "Let Michael do it," Mrs. J commanded. "He's better than you. Thank God I don't have to be your teacher." Margaret gave way to Michael. "I'm so stupid, aren't I, Mom?" Mrs. J agreed.

In discussing the children, Mrs. J drew contrasting profiles. Margaret is like a teenager – asking for makeup and thinking about sex too much. "She ignores me when I tell her to stay in her room." Mrs. J reported feeling so angry at Margaret that she was afraid of losing control – "I could beat her up. I could kill her. I tell her I'll give her to her father, but he probably wouldn't want her. I hate her."

Mrs. J had a different image of Michael. "He's very likable. He has many friends. He really seems to know what I like. One time he even spent all of his allowance to buy me some earrings. He's a real man type. At times he can be moody. He and Margaret fight. They are poison to each other."

In her interview, Margaret could say nothing about her mother that she liked. "She treats me like s---." Michael volunteered an explanation of his mother's behavior: "My mother is in a bad mood because she is sick and usually because of my sister."

In the next year, there were more family changes. Because of the severity of Mrs. J's illness, custody of the children was transferred to Mr. J. The children visited their mother. The visits frequently ended in terrible scenes of anger. The move to their father's house meant that the children were separated from all the children they knew, and they were transferred to another school.

Mr. J found his responsibilities overwhelming. He hired a woman to be in the house from the close of the school day to when he got home from work. The children didn't like her and got into shouting matches. Their school problems escalated. Mr. J described the children's moods as alternating: When one was cooperative, the other was angry and oppositional. Never any peace. He was so frustrated, he ended up spanking Margaret. He tried being playful and affectionate with both children, but had no success in managing them.

At 10 years and 8½ years, Margaret and Michael were seen again at the apartment, with their father. Margaret was extremely talkative, frequently asking inappropriate questions. Her moods fluctuated from friendly and cooperative, as she was responding to the psychiatric interview, to agitated activity, inability to sit still, pouting and frowning. Finally she broke into crying and a tantrum. She then withdrew to TV watching.

Michael is large for his age. He was ill-at-ease, but with a steady flow of irritability and oppositionality, he accepted interview procedures.

Things had improved at home. Mr. J had found a better apartment and the three of them were for once happily getting resettled. No school changes were necessary. Margaret was especially pleased. She now seldom visited her mother. Her mother begged to take her out for an evening at the movies. The evening ended up badly with Mrs. J becoming manic and driving out in the country for several hours until she was stopped by the police for "drunken driving." Mrs. J was taken to the hospital. Margaret was at the police station until her father came to get her.

Michael continued to visit his mother after she got out of the hospital. He would cook and clean with her. She found him very "loyal." She was pleased that he was big. "He's a push and shove kind of guy. He's got a good head on his shoulders."

Michael's father describes him as very stubborn, impatient, fidgety. He doesn't make any effort to see friends. Unless he is given something to do, he ends up watching TV: "He hasn't many friends because he is so involved with the family's problems. He feels responsible for his mother."

"Margaret can be very good when you are alone with her," her father said. "She's outgoing, active, and chipper. She's very uplifting." (These are similar descriptions Mr. J gave of his wife about the early years of their marriage.) "She's kinder and easier to live with. She got better after she saw her mother really sick. She understands more."

Margaret edged into adolescence at an early age. When father and children next came to the apartment, Margaret was 13. She had become overweight and looked ultramature – excessive makeup, short, short skirt.

For the past year, her school performance had been a problem, and she had been placed in a special class. She's been going with what her father calls a bad crowd. She is going around with an 18-year-old girl, who is very much a loner. She has stayed out all night.

In her interviews, Margaret required constant encouragement and attention to keep her attention and motivation. She was concerned that she might have her mother's illness. She asked repeatedly, "Do I have bipolar?" "Is it in me?" She reported that she worried about everything. She would get up at 4:30 to do her hair. "I don't want to do it wrong." "I can get sad very easily. Even if I have a pimple, I will cry." But she reassured herself, "but I don't think I'm God like my mother."

Michael at 11½ was hyper. His speech was pressured and he showed a racing kind of imagination. He did well in school academically but was expelled for smoking. He felt motivated to do well. He feels he understands about his mother's illness; at the same time he says that her energy just means she is having fun.

FAMILY S

Jenny was born at home, the product of an apparently healthy pregnancy and delivery. The birth was captured on the family's new video camera, and Mrs. S, despite her premonitions that another girl would be as difficult as the first one, described how much closer she felt to this "good and easy baby" that slept many hours.

By contrast, her first girl had been somewhat of a disappointment. Mrs. S had been hoping for a boy who would be born at home by natural childbirth and, instead, Martha was born by cesarean section in the hospital and required a hospital stay of a week due to fever.

Mrs. S did not have good memories of Martha during the first

1½ years of life. She was active, required little sleep, and kept her parents busy. Although Mrs. S remembered feeling overwhelmed by Martha, Mr. S was eager to help with the child, and a special bond developed between them.

Both parents were well-intentioned, successful individuals who planned to raise children in the best possible environment. Mrs. S had knowledge of child development and worked in a daycare center before the children were born. Both parents wanted to raise their children differently from the way they had been raised. The maternal grandmother had died when Mrs. S was only 5 years old. An authoritarian, stiff paternal aunt became her adoptive mother. After her mother's death, her father was mostly absent. She moved and changed schools frequently, making it difficult for her to make friends. She recalled that changes made her feel depressed, and at times she thought of suicide to escape her emotions and pain.

Mr. S's mother had been hospitalized for bipolar illness, multiple times while he was growing up. A younger sister became depressed during adolescence and attempted suicide. He grew up familiar with depression, and helping his wife when she was depressed seemed natural for him.

When we met the family for the first home visit, the father explained that Mrs. S had slipped back into deep depression. He had been waiting for the psychiatrist to call with advice. Mr. S was interested in our research and welcomed the diversion of a visit.

Mrs. S was sitting on the sofa in the sunny family room. She nodded at the introduction, but turned back to Jenny, avoiding further eye contact. Jenny was lying close to her mother noisily sucking her thumb and occasionally giving a whimper while she clung to her blanket. She didn't look up to notice the new toys that we brought even though Martha was playing happily with them with her father. Mrs. S gulped air as she blinked her eyes – holding back tears – and then her eyes glazed over while she rubbed Jenny's leg, soothing herself and Jenny. Mother and child seemed to be immersed in the same depressive state.

A second home visit was arranged a few weeks later when Mrs.

S seemed better. Jenny and Martha were standing at the door, excited. Mrs. S came to the door with a friendly greeting. Later, she volunteered a tour of her children's room and play area in the basement. It was evident that she had spent time and thought in designing a creative learning atmosphere. She wanted to be a "perfect" mother but felt swamped by the daily laundry and endless dishes. Most of all she felt despair – a failure when the children did not respond as she wished. Mrs. S felt that her girls took turns in harassing her by whining and demanding special food or treatment and by purposefully misbehaving (i.e., climbing on the kitchen table and jumping off).

Several weeks later, Jenny, not quite 3 years old, and her mother drove up the big tree-covered hill to the large Tudor house that is the laboratory. For many children, the entrance – high ceilings, wood-paneled walls and an imposing spiral staircase – is a novel setting. Some children draw close to their mother and hold a hand for security, but Jenny clung to her mother and demanded to be carried into the house and up the stairs. Mother and child were molded together as one. Jenny seemed not to look at anyone, or at the toys. Jenny's face was expressionless. She became very upset when her mother briefly left the room. She whined constantly during the morning. She trailed her blanket along as her mother tried to find some activity to interest her. Nothing satisfied her. Mrs. S tried to cheer her with food but she pushed it away. Finally when she accepted some juice, she took a large gulp, holding the juice in her mouth while watching for her mother's reaction. It seemed like a familiar pattern between mother and child: mother urging her to swallow before she choked, Jenny refusing for many minutes, followed by a choke and an explosion of juice. Despite her distress, Mrs. S picked up Jenny and held her, as if she were a little baby, and walked back and forth, Jenny sucking her thumb and clutching her blanket.

During the 6-week period over which the laboratory visits were scheduled, Mrs. S was fighting a deep depression. She was hospitalized for 2 weeks after becoming unable to function. An adjustment of medications and sessions with her psychiatrist seemed to help and she returned to the laboratory.

Mrs. S's mood varied during the visit and between visits in a way that could only seem confusing to her children. At times she was withdrawn and unresponsive, then very affectionate and playing creative games with them. At times she was sad, fighting back tears as she read a story to the children. At other times she was overwrought, anxiously fidgeting as she chain-smoked. She said that she expected the worst from her children, expecting that one or the other would torment her. She became annoyed at the demanding, clinging, whining of Jenny, and at Martha's constant bickering, fussing, and meddling with Jenny. Her ability to set limits fluctuated.

At the visit shared by Jenny and Martha (age 5), mother was at her best. She was relaxed and cheerful, neatly groomed and in control of herself. The children responded to this change in their mother by playing cooperatively and happily.

During the psychiatric play interview, Jenny's moods seemed to fluctuate more than the moods of most children her age. At times she was withdrawn and unresponsive. Her face was expressionless, or she looked sad and forlorn. She could also respond with smiles and appropriate answers. At times she became frantic, with a nervous laughter that went "beyond happy."

The family was called for their second period of assessment, about 3 years after the first assessment. It was a shock to learn that the mother had committed suicide about a year after we had last seen her. Mr. S said that all seemed to have gone along better until the winter when both girls had been sick with colds and flu for months. The day of her death, she had sent the children to school as usual.

Mr. S blamed himself for the tragedy and became depressed himself and withdrew into his work. He tried to help the girls by providing diversion, such as gymnastics or dance lessons, and would take them on an occasional bike ride.

In the follow-up assessment, Jenny (age 6½) impressed everyone by her open friendly manner with adults. During the psychiatric interview, she gave a factual account of her mother's death, and claimed that she had no memory of her mother. She did remember the first Nanny, whom she described as very mean and showing preference for Martha.

At this time, despite Jenny's general friendly manner, she was very anxious. She had intense fears that her father might not come home, or that her grandmother might die. She was afraid that a monster would break her window and steal her away, or that she might get lost in the crowd, or that the house might burn down. She also described to the clinician that when things did not go as she wanted, she had plans to run away. Three times she had taken the wagon and walked around a long block, although she was scared. After arguments with Martha, she would run out of the house, yelling.

She was still wetting the bed and sucking her thumb. Her father reported that she complained frequently of stomachaches. She chewed her hands and picked mosquito bites until they were deep sores. Her tendency was to blame herself.

Although she tried to be "nice" to the children at school, she was not liked by them. At home she retreated to her bedroom where she could keep things in order. She drew endless brick houses, carefully, each brick drawn separately and lined up evenly.

Martha was very aware of her feelings about her mother's death. She reported feeling very sad. She had many worries. She had adopted a maternal role with Jenny and talked about being upset at her sister for running away.

The family returned to the laboratory when Jenny was 10 and Martha was 12 years old. By this time, Mr. S was remarried, and his new wife had moved in with the family. Both children had difficulty accepting her.

Jenny still wet her bed, no longer tried to make friends, and obsessed about small injuries. Martha's concerns centered around her perfectionism. She wanted to please adults. She was a follower of her peers, wanting desperately to fit in, to be accepted by them.

When Jenny returned for the fourth follow-up, she reviewed the problems of the past, and the way she felt connected to her mother's depressive history. For the past 2 years, she found herself becoming depressed in the winter, the time of her mother's death. She recalled seeing her mother's casket and her father sobbing.

Jenny remembered her family's complaints about her, as being whiny and selfish. Like her mother, she would chew her fingernails until they became infected. Currently the issue in the family was about getting her to eat. Jenny had been hospitalized for a month for anorexia. She said she felt like running away.

A year and a half later, Jenny's father called to report that Jenny had become deeply depressed, and had again been hospitalized. She was diagnosed there as "bipolar, borderline personality." She met a boy in the hospital who taught her how to run away. Her father could not find her. She lived in the woods, or camped on the floor at a friend's house. She had an abortion in the past year.

Adolescence was turbulent for Martha, also. She rebelled continuously, an angry teenager. To make a point, she scratched her wrist with a razor. She claimed that she had no intention of committing suicide, but the authorities at school and her father reacted with panic and arranged therapy. Martha was depressed and lethargic: she had gained 30 pounds. During the worst period she couldn't get out of bed. She had trouble keeping friends. Martha started college, living about 1 hour from home, but she dropped out by Christmastime because she could not adjust to the stress.

6

THE DEVELOPMENT OF
CHILDREN OF DEPRESSED
AND WELL MOTHERS:
GROUP ANALYSES

Our investigation of the links between parental psychopathology and psychopathology in the offspring begins descriptively with a search into the psychiatric and psychosocial functioning of the children as it is related to the broad distinction of affectively ill and psychiatrically well mothers. We will not pause at this point to consider the complexity and heterogeneity involved in this classification of parents. Initially we are focusing on maternal diagnosis (unipolar depression, bipolar illness, or no psychiatric diagnosis) as the conditions associated with varied offspring outcomes. We have imposed a developmental analysis on this issue. Many of the questions we are investigating in these group descriptions we are asking repeatedly throughout the book, increasingly bringing into our analyses considerations of maternal complexity and multiple interacting factors influencing offspring.

PORTRAITS OF DEVELOPMENT THROUGH CHILDHOOD: CROSS-SECTIONAL ANALYSES OF PSYCHIATRIC ASSESSMENTS

Our first presentations are group portraits of the children of depressed and well mothers. The problems illustrated in the case studies in chapter 5 are generalized here into developmental

59

group profiles, and referenced to normal developmental capabilities and demands.

Psychiatric assessments of the children are in terms of the three clusters of symptoms – depressive disorders, anxiety disorders, and disruptive–oppositional disorders and a summary assessment – a problem in any cluster and/or somatic disorders, substance abuse, or anorexia. All of the measures are categorical.

The categorical WLS approach is used. Preplanned contrasts are always included, comparing each pair of mother diagnosis groups. The significance of the main effects of mother diagnosis and gender of the child and their interaction are all evaluated. When the interaction is significant, indicating different effects of mother diagnosis within the two genders, the effect of the mother's diagnosis within each gender is examined. (Findings relating to gender are discussed in chapter 13.)

The group profiles of children's problems, from toddlerhood to early adolescence, are presented in Figures 6.1 to 6.4. The related statistical comparisons are shown in Table 6.1.

Toddler to Preschool Age (1½ to 3½ Years) (see Fig. 6.1)

The *children of well mothers* conform to normative expectations for this age. Their problematic behavior is primarily anxious behavior (30% of children), mainly age-expected separation anxiety. It is doubtful that separation anxiety at this age qualifies as deviant behavior, although some of the children manifest extremes of this behavior. Disruptive–oppositional behavior, although not unexpected at 2 and 3 years, characterizes few of the children (16.7%). No child of a well mother, at this age, presents problematic depressed affect. Two-thirds of the children have a secure attachment relationship. The overall group profile is consistent with the literature in finding that young children from favorable backgrounds are not without difficulties in mastering developmental tasks (Campbell, 1989), but they are, for the most part, meeting the socialization demands of this age period.

The *children of mothers with bipolar illness* present a mixed picture of adaptive and problematic behavior. On psychiatric assessments, most of these children are seen as nonproblematic. They separate readily from mother and relate easily to the clinician. Only 12% are described as anxious and another 12% (not the same children) are oppositional. None shows depressive affect. There is, however, the disturbing coexistence of insecure attachment, measured by the Strange Situation, in 60% of these children, predominantly disorganized attachment. Their ready separation from the mother to join the psychiatrist does not appear to derive from their security of attachment. For some of these children, this discrepancy between their positive and "mature" responding in the relatively superficial relationships with adults and their functioning in the intimate relationship with mother marks a provocative beginning of a developmental path.

The psychiatrist conducting the play interviews (blind to mother's diagnosis and to the attachment relationship) saw the children as confident. He predicted a positive developmental course for 63% of the children of bipolar mothers, compared with similar predictions for 36% of the children of well mothers, and 24% of the children of unipolar mothers. With their nonstressed engagement in the psychiatric session and their easy and pleasant contacts with the clinician, these children appeared socially skilled.

The young *children of unipolar mothers* present a different combination of characteristics. Separation anxiety is frequent (33% of the children), as is disruptive–oppositional behavior (33% of the children). Three children of unipolar mothers show signs of extreme depressed affect and behavior. Of the children of unipolar mothers, 38% are insecurely attached. Children in this group were not singled out as socially skillful.

Early Childhood (5 to 7 years) (see Fig. 6.2)

Children of both sibling groups were seen in the early school years. Normatively, children of this age will have adapted to the increased demands for behavioral control at home and in school,

Table 6.1 *Psychiatric assessment of children's problems, by mother's diagnosis and age of child*

Age of child	Sibling cohort	Child problem	Generalized Wald statistics (χ^2)			
			Overall df = 2 (*p*)	Contrasts df = 1 (*p*)		
				Well vs. bipolar	Well vs. unipolar	Bipolar vs. unipolar
1½ to 3½	Younger	Anxious	6.49 (<.05)	3.36 (<.10)	n.s.[a]	5.48 (<.05)
		Depressed	n.s.			
		Disruptive–oppositional	5.58 (<.10)	n.s.	2.87 (<.10)	5.35 (<.05)
		Any of above	8.32 (<.05)	n.s.	n.s.	8.32 (<.01)
5 to 6	Younger	Anxious	n.s.			
		Depressed	16.69 (<.001)	5.53 (<.05)	13.16 (<.001)	n.s.
		Disruptive–oppositional	4.96 (<.10)	3.76 (<.10)	n.s.	n.s.
		Any of above	10.67 (<.01)	n.s.	10.67 (<.01)	n.s.
		Any problem	5.71 (<.10)	n.s.	5.51 (<.05)	n.s.
5 to 8	Older	Anxious	n.s.			
		Depressed	5.29 (<.10)		5.21 (<.05)	n.s.
		Disruptive–oppositional	n.s.			
		Any of above	7.99 (<.05)	n.s.	7.06 (<.01)	
		Any problem	8.26 (<.05)	n.s.	7.60 (<.01)	

62

Age	Group	Problem				
8 to 11	Younger	Anxious	6.49 (<.05)	n.s.	6.46 (<.05)	n.s.
		Depressed	n.s.			
		Disruptive–oppositional	7.02 (<.05)	n.s.	6.43 (<.05)	n.s.
		Any of above	9.56 (<.01)	n.s.	9.46 (<.01)	n.s.
		Any problem	10.37 (<.01)	n.s.	10.37 (<.01)	n.s.
8 to 11	Older	Anxious	n.s.			
		Depressed	16.34 (<.001)	6.13 (<.05)	13.90 (<.001)	n.s.
		Disruptive–oppositional	25.17 (<.001)	3.24 (<.10)	24.00 (<.0001)	4.46 (<.05)
		Any of above	13.35 (<.01)	n.s.	13.08 (<.001)	2.81 (<.10)
		Any problem	13.14 (<.01)	5.47 (<.05)	12.80 (<.001)	n.s.
11 to 15	Older	Anxious	8.93 (<.05)	4.39 (<.05)	7.40 (<.01)	n.s.
		Depressed	12.52 (<.01)	10.68 (<.01)	5.34 (<.05)	n.s.
		Disruptive–oppositional	n.s.			
		Any of above	9.28 (<.01)	5.47 (<.05)	8.18 (<.01)	n.s.
		Any problem	9.26 (<.01)	5.47 (<.05)	8.18 (<.01)	n.s.

[a] n.s.: not significant.

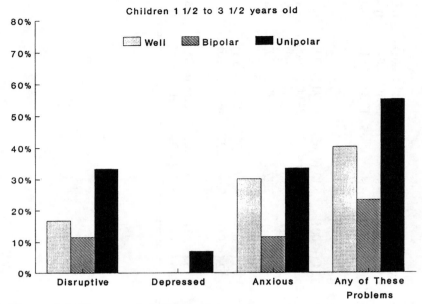

Figure 6.1. Percent of children with each psychiatric problem by mother's diagnosis; younger sibling cohort.

and will have succeeded in separating briefly from mother without great distress.

The *children of well mothers* generally conform to age expectations. Relatively few have anxiety problems (16.7% and 13.3% of younger and older siblings, respectively) or disruptive problems (6.7% and 10.0% of younger and older siblings, respectively). Surprisingly, pronounced depressed affect appears in one child of a well mother in the younger sibling cohort and four children in the older sibling cohort.

Children of bipolar mothers, as in the preschool period, show low rates of anxiety disorders (11.5% of younger and 9.1% of older siblings). They make a substantial showing of disruptive behavior (23.1% and 22.7% in the younger and older siblings, respectively). Depressive symptoms (23.1% and 18.2%) appear, where no depressive symptoms were present at the younger age.

More than half of the *5- to 7-year-olds of unipolar mothers* are pre-

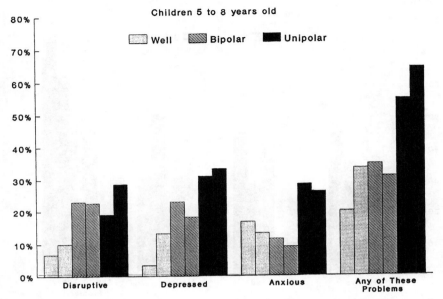

Figure 6.2. Percent of children with each psychiatric problem by mother's diagnosis. For each bar pair: left bar is younger cohort; right bar is older cohort.

senting some kind of problem (54.8% of the younger and 64.3% of the older siblings). Their problems are disruptive disorders (19.0% and 28.6%) and/or depressive problems (31% and 33%), and/or anxiety (primarily separation anxiety) (28.6% and 26.2%, respectively).

Middle Childhood (8 to 11 years) (see Fig. 6.3)

The *children of well parents* show little change in their diagnostic pattern. Approximately a third have some problem. Overanxious behavior and separation anxiety account for many of their diagnoses.

These childhood years bring diagnosed problems to nearly half of the *children of bipolar mothers,* and to two-thirds of the *children of unipolar mothers.* Their problems appear in all of the areas.

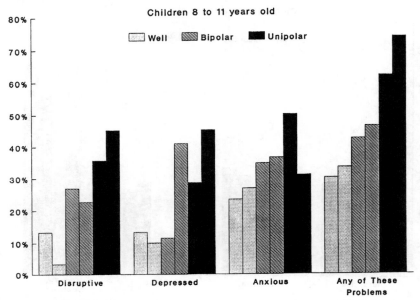

Figure 6.3. Percent of children with each psychiatric problem by mother's diagnosis. For each bar pair: left bar is younger cohort; right bar is older cohort.

Rather than meeting maturity expectations, these children have clearly lost ground.

Early Adolescence (11 to 15 Years) (see Fig. 6.4)

In early adolescence, the profiles of the *children of bipolar and unipolar mothers* show high rates of problems (57.7% in the bipolar and 69% in the unipolar group). *Children of well mothers* have problems in about a third of the cases. The profiles of the children of well and depressed mothers have clearly separated.

Summary of Group Differences

From this descriptive account, we see that, in the earliest years, the offspring of unipolar, bipolar, and well mothers present dis-

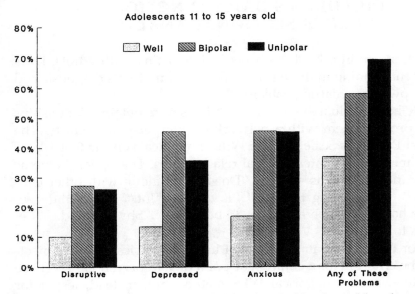

Figure 6.4. Percent of children with each psychiatric problem by mother's diagnosis; older sibling cohort.

tinct configurations of affect and relationships. They are negotiating the age-characteristic struggles quite differently. The children of unipolar depressed mothers appear more problematic than the children of bipolar depressed and well mothers. However, the configuration in the children of bipolar mothers (of insecurity in relating to the mother and easy, nonanxious relationships with others) deviates from a normal pattern.

From these chartings of problems in childhood it is evident that psychiatric outcomes in later adolescence and early maturity have diverse predecessors. To learn the sequences of problems and individual differences in paths, longitudinal records are needed. Before examining these differences in detail in longitudinal analyses, we continue the cross-sectional portraits to examine children's everyday functioning.

CHILDREN'S DAILY FUNCTIONING: CROSS-SECTIONAL ANALYSES

Children are in school, with peers, interacting with adults. Does their functioning in these roles reflect their mother's diagnosis and their own psychiatric problems?

We have evaluated children's abilities to maintain relationships that provide them with a network of interpersonal security. The Social Problems Scale and the Withdrawn Scale on the CBCL provide measures of interpersonal relationships. The Social Problems Scale includes items such as "Doesn't get along with other children," "Acts young for age," "Is teased a lot." The Withdrawn Scale has items such as "Likes to be alone," "Shy or timid," "Refuses to talk."

(For the CBCL data, because of low frequencies of scores meeting the criterion for a clinical cut-point of 90th percentile, we chose not to use the categorical WLS method but, instead, tested for homogeneity among the mother diagnosis groups and between the genders in two independent analyses, employing Fisher's Exact Test.)

Maternal diagnosis makes a difference. Children of depressed mothers, more often than children of well mothers (see Table 6.2), have clinically high scores on one or both of the scales, indicating difficulties in relationships. Differences appear at all age levels, beginning at 5–8 years. On a second measure made at the end of childhood, ratings of the children's peer relationships based on combined mother and teacher descriptions support these findings. Peer relationships are rated as poor for 42% of the children of bipolar mothers, 45% of the children of unipolar mothers, and 17% of the children of well mothers in the older cohort (χ^2 (2) = 17.15, $p < .001$). A similar (statistically nonsignificant) pattern appears in the younger group (35% of children of bipolar mothers, 31% of children of unipolar mothers, and 17% of children of well mothers).

Children's self-reports further confirm difficulties in relating to others. Interestingly, 42% of the children of bipolar mothers and

Table 6.2 *Percentage of children with problems of clinical concern: CBCL narrow-band scales, by mother's diagnosis and age of child*

Age of child	Child's problem	Younger siblings				Older siblings			
		Well mother	Bipolar mother	Unipolar mother	p^a	Well mother	bipolar mother	Unipolar mother	p
5–7	Social problems	0.0	12.0	9.5	n.s.^{b}	0.0	9.1	16.7	<.05
	Withdrawn	0.0	16.6	16.7	<.05	3.3	18.2	14.3	n.s.
8–11	Social problems	0.0	19.2	19.5	<.05	0.0	4.6	18.9	<.05
	Withdrawn	0.0	3.9	17.1	<.05	3.6	13.6	32.4	<.01
11–15	Social problems					0.0	9.1	11.9	n.s.
	Withdrawn					0.0	15.8	16.7	<.05

[a]Fisher's Exact Probability with 2 df.
[b]n.s.: not significant.

37% of the children of unipolar mothers describe themselves as annoying to others (DICA question). Only 10% of the children of well mothers accept this description of themselves.

How well do the children fulfill a central job requirement of childhood, namely, succeeding in school? The academic and behavioral requirements of school are more poorly met by the children of depressed mothers. In the younger group, 23%, 17%, and 0% of children of bipolar, unipolar, and well mothers, respectively, are doing very poorly in school ($\chi^2 = 17.15$, $p < .001$). A similar (statistically nonsignificant) pattern appears in the older group: 23%, 19%, and 10% of the children of bipolar, unipolar, and well mother groups, respectively.

Self-concepts (Harter scale) assessed in middle and late childhood show little relation to maternal diagnosis. Children in the younger group did not differ in self-concept as a function of maternal diagnosis. Where a higher score denotes better self-concepts, mean scores and standard deviations are 12.95 (2.1), 11.73 (1.5), and 12.07 (1.9) for the older children of well, bipolar, and unipolar depressed mothers, respectively, (F(2,87) = 3.12, $p < .05$).

In the overall picture of daily functioning, the children of ill mothers are giving considerable evidence of problems. If the child is failing in even one area, he/she is functionally handicapped in day-to-day experiences. There are children who are failing in multiple areas, and again they are the children of ill mothers. Failures in multiple areas characterize 27%, 12%, and 0% of the younger children and 30%, 29%, and 3% of older siblings of bipolar, unipolar, and well mothers, respectively.

Psychiatric Diagnoses and Daily Functioning

We should expect to find that the children with diagnoses are also the children who are failing in social relationships, self-concept, and school performance. While this tends to be the case, it is unevenly so (see Table 6.3). Children without a diagnosis are functioning adequately in three-fourths of the cases, and few are failing in multiple areas. The greatest impairments in daily functioning appear in children who have diagnoses of both internalizing and externalizing problems. Only 39% and 19% of the younger and older siblings are functioning well. This group stands out in impairments in all three areas of functioning.

Not to be overlooked is the high proportion (more than half) of the children with diagnoses of internalizing disorders only who are functioning adaptively, with good school performance, a network of peers, and a positive self-concept. There may well be costs, however, that are not evident in these data.

LONGITUDINAL ANALYSES OF OFFSPRING PROBLEMS

The preceding analyses have provided cross-sectional and summary appraisals of the children. We turn now to longitudinal analyses that allow us to sharpen the questions of development.

Repeated Measures

Through a repeated measures design, we are addressing three questions. The first is: Do children in the three maternal groups differ in the proportion exhibiting a problem, when all three assessment periods are considered; that is, is one group more prone to a particular problem than another group, even if not at a given age? (main effect of mother's diagnosis?). The repeated measures analyses (see Table 6.4) support and strengthen what was seen in the cross-sectional analyses. The effect of maternal diagnosis is significant for each of the three cluster diagnoses and for "any" diagnosed problem, in both sibling groups. Children of unipolar mothers have significantly more problems in all categories than do children of well mothers, when time (development) is not considered.

Significantly fewer of the younger children of bipolar mothers have diagnosed problems of depression than do children of unipolar mothers. There are fewer diagnoses of anxiety and "any" problems than among children of unipolar mothers. In this pre-

71

Table 6.3 *Percentage of children with zero, one, or more areas of problems in daily functioning, by child's diagnosis at Time 3*

Sibling cohort	Child's problems[a]	Number of problem areas				Wald χ^2
		n	0	1	2 or 3	
Younger 8 to 11 years	No diagnosis	44	77.3	18.2	4.6	12.31
	Depressed, alone or with other internalizing	7	57.1	42.9	0.0	p<.05
	Internalizing and externalizing	23	39.1	30.4	30.4	
	Anxious, alone or with somatic problems	21	61.9	19.1	19.1	
	Externalizing only	3	66.7	33.3	0.0	
Older 11 to 15 years	No diagnosis	39	74.4	15.4	10.3	34.60
	Depressed, alone or with other internalizing	18	50.0	27.8	22.2	p<.0001
	Internalizing and externalizing	16	18.8	12.5	68.8	
	Anxious, alone or with somatic problems	17	58.8	35.3	5.9	
	Externalizing only	4	0.00	75.0	25.0	

[a]Each child problem group was contrasted with the no diagnosis group. Significant contrasts for the younger cohort: No diagnosis vs. internalizing and externalizing, $\chi^2 = 11.05$, $p < .001$. For the older cohort: No diagnosis vs. internalizing and externalizing, $\chi^2 = 24.71$, $p < .0001$; no diagnosis vs. internalizing only, $\chi^2 = 13.68$, $p < .001$.

Table 6.4 Repeated measures analyses of child psychiatric problems

Cohort	Child diagnosis	Wald χ² — Main effect of mother's diagnosis df = 2 (p)	Time df = 2 (p)	Time within mother's diagnosis[a] df = 2 (p)	Contrasts df = 1 (p) — Well vs. unipolar	Well vs. bipolar	Bipolar vs. unipolar
Younger	Depressed	58.79 (<.0001)		− Bipolar 8.53 (<.05) Unipolar 12.73 (<.01) Well 4.61 (<.10)	50.79 (<.0001)	8.14 (<.01)	4.40 (<.05)
	Anxious	10.24 (.01)	9.6 (<.01)		6.13 (<.05)	n.s.	8.84 (<.01)
	Externalizing	8.24 (<.05)	n.s.[b]		8.05 (<.01)	n.s.	n.s.
	Any of above	18.83 (<.001)	n.s.		17.36 (<.0001)	n.s.	n.s.
	Any problem	16.00 (<.001)	n.s.		14.01 (<.001)	n.s.	8.40 (<.001)
Older	Depressed	25.10 (<.001)	n.s.		18.79 (<.0001)	8.60 (<.01)	n.s.
	Anxious	7.12 (<.05)	12.05 (<.01)		6.94 (<.01)	n.s.	n.s.
	Externalizing	21.40 (<.0001)	n.s.		20.59 (<.0001)	4.02 (<.05)	n.s.
	Any of above	24.46 (<.0001)	n.s.		24.43 (<.001)	3.99 (<.05)	3.26 (<.10)
	Any problem	24.75 (<.0001)	n.s.		24.74 (<.0001)	6.61 (<.01)	n.s.

[a] For depressed younger children the significant interaction of mother's diagnosis by time was replaced with the effect of time within each mother diagnosis.

[b] n.s.: not significant.

pubertal age span (up to 11 years), the offspring of bipolar mothers do not stand out as a highly problematic group.

This cannot be said of the older children of bipolar mothers (age span 5–8 to 11–15 years). They, in contrast, significantly more often have diagnoses of depression, disruption, and "any" diagnosed problem, but not anxiety, than do children of well mothers. The older children of bipolar mothers do not differ significantly from children of unipolar mothers.

We next ask whether some problems are more likely at one age than another (main effect of time). Also, are the groups equally different (or alike) at each age in the proportion of children with a particular problem, or do the groups differ more at one age than another? A query might be whether the groups are similar in early childhood and become increasingly more disparate, or are some groups much higher in problem rates from early childhood on (maternal diagnosis by time interactions)?

Anxiety changes significantly with development. It appears at a moderate level at the youngest age (separation anxiety), drops to its lowest level at age 5 to 7, and rises to higher levels again at succeeding ages.

The maternal diagnosis by time interaction is significant only for depression. Among the younger children of depressed mothers, the percentage with a diagnosis rises significantly between the preschool age and age 5 to 7. It does not change significantly in the well group.

Survival Analyses

The survival analyses inform us of the rates at which children of each maternal group acquire each diagnosis. The rate is the proportion of new cases of a problem appearing within a given time frame. A high rate is equivalent to many new cases. The proportion of children who have never had the problem is plotted through childhood and into adolescence (T4) (see Fig. 6.5).

The rate of development of problems of depression is highest for children of unipolar mothers and lowest in children of well mothers. Results of the Log-rank test are $\chi^2(2) = 15.96$, $p <$

.0005 for the younger children and $\chi^2(2) = 13.06$, $p < .005$ for the older group.

By the time of the last assessment, problems of depression have appeared at some time in the course of development in 42%, 62%, and 17% of younger siblings, and in 73%, 76%, and 37% of the older children of bipolar, unipolar, and well mothers, respectively. The proportion of children of depressed mothers remaining free of depression drops markedly. In the children of well mothers, the proportion declines only slightly over time.

The rate of development of disruptive–oppositional problems differs among the maternal groups at a trend level in the younger group $\chi^2(2) = 4.84$, $p < .09$), and significantly in the older group ($\chi^2(2) = 18.30$, $p < .0001$). Children of unipolar mothers have the fastest rate, and children of well mothers the slowest rate. By the time of the last assessment, 47%, 60%, and 33% of the younger siblings, and 54%, 71%, and 20% of the older siblings of mothers of bipolar, unipolar, and well mothers, respectively, have exhibited disruptive problems. Few new cases of disruption occur in adolescence, except in the children of bipolar mothers.

The rate of development of anxiety problems also differs by maternal diagnosis (Log-rank $\chi^2(2) = 7.41$, $p < .05$, younger cohort; $\chi^2(2) = 7.57$, $p < .05$, older cohort). The rate is faster in children of unipolar mothers than in the other groups. Anxiety develops at a slower rate in the younger children of bipolar mothers. By the last assessment, 46%, 76%, and 60% of the younger children of bipolar, unipolar, and well mothers, respectively, have had anxiety problems. The parallel figures in the older children are 64%, 79%, and 43%.

The rate of development of "any" problem summarizes development. Most children have a problem at some time. Children of unipolar mothers show the fastest rate of problem development.

SUMMARY

The cross-sectional and longitudinal descriptions of offspring problems furnish information on the influences of two major variables,

75

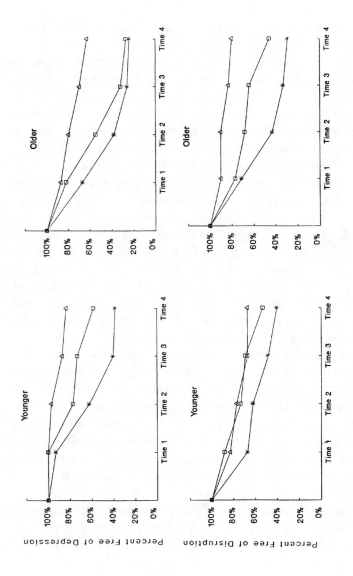

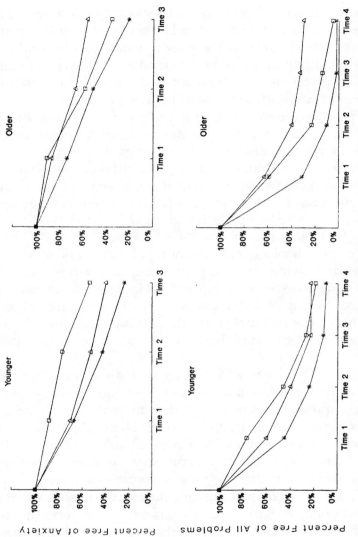

Figure 6.5. Survival functions: Percentage of children remaining free of problem at each time of assessment, for depression, disruption, anxiety, and "any" problem, as a function of mother's diagnosis. (Δ) Well; (□) bipolar; (*) unipolar.

77

maternal depression and developmental stage. The findings replicate the research literature on elevated rates of problems in the offspring of depressed mothers. The present study goes beyond this finding by identifying the role of development in the content and frequency of problems. Development is different for children of well, unipolar depressed, and bipolar depressed mothers.

Seeing *how* it is different begins to build the knowledge that is necessary for an understanding of the processes involved in the emergence of psychopathology. The findings that maternal unipolar depression and bipolar illness have different associations with offspring behavior, at different developmental stages, suggest new questions and hypotheses relevant to both etiology and intervention for these two offspring groups.

What is to explain the special "sparkle" and "maturity" of a subgroup of preschool-age children of bipolar mothers? What are the factors underlying the sharp upswing in problems in late childhood and adolescence in children of bipolar mothers, and the early and continuing disturbances in many of the children of unipolar mothers? The fact that so much goes on in the prepubertal years invites investigation of this period as precursor to later psychopathology.

The childhood problems of offspring of depressed mothers are not confined to depressive disorders, or even dominated by them. This raises questions concerning determinants of children's "choices" of problem. Or, are the other problems (disruption and anxiety) early phases of disorder that eventually evolve into depression? Further, we see early depressive disorders appearing sometimes with conduct problems, and sometimes alone or with anxiety. These different patterns are differently related to children's functioning in such critical areas as school performance, peer relationships, and concepts of the self. Etiologically these children may differ, and prognostically they may be on different paths.

7

THE DEVELOPMENT OF CHILDREN OF DEPRESSED AND WELL MOTHERS: LONGITUDINAL ANALYSES OF INDIVIDUAL DEVELOPMENT

The longitudinal approach holds out the tempting goal of understanding or explaining individual developmental processes. The group analyses have documented developmental patterns in content, timing, and frequencies of children's problems related to mother's depression. We wish now to identify individuality within these patterns, and to represent the organization of the child's maladaptive and adaptive functioning over time.

With the individual child as the focus, it is possible to address questions concerning continuities and changes. How do problems evolve in the child over time? Are some problems preludes to other kinds of problems?

INDIVIDUAL DEVELOPMENTAL PROBLEM PATHS

To trace the sequence of each diagnostic cluster and "any" problem, each child was coded into one of the following paths.

1. The problem appears in the first six years and (a) is confined to that period, (b) recurs later (not continual), or (c) is continual (3 or 4 assessment periods).

79

2. The problem first appears in middle childhood (8 to 11 years) and (a) is confined to that period or (b) recurs after age 11.

3. The problem first appears in adolescence (for younger cohort, 11 to 15; for older cohort, 11 to 19 years).

As we see from the plotted pathways shown in Tables 7.1 and 7.2 children travel through childhood with problems appearing at various ages, variously transient and recurrent. At whatever point in time we assess children, the problems appearing at that time, in different children, are likely to be at various stages in the history or path of the problem: a new problem, a continuing problem, a problem about to be resolved or to evolve into a different problem. Although these differences are taken into account clinically, in research, we often lose this relevant information. The consequence is that we are then seeking common explanations of children who are at quite different stages in their functioning.

Across maternal diagnostic groups, children differ in the paths of problems over time in each of the problem areas. Based on the criterion of "any" problem, many children begin a problem path in the first six years, regardless of mother's diagnosis. They exhibit behavior sufficiently "deviant" to be of clinical concern (see Table 7.1, rows 2, 3, and 7; 60%, 54%, and 76% of children of well, bipolar, and unipolar mothers, respectively). The problems at this age, we assume, reflect a high component of normative disregulation. However, the fates of these early failures are very different in children of well and of depressed mothers. Children of well mothers are likely to have resolved many of these early problems when we see them three years later. Of those who began with problems before age 6, 61% (11 of 18) no longer have problems. Quite the opposite is the case for the children of depressed mothers. Only 14% (2 of 14) and 16% (5 of 42) of the children of bipolar and unipolar mothers who presented problems before age 6 return without problems 3 and/or 6 years later. For reasons of either early inherent vulnerabilities or inadequacies in early rearing conditions (examined later), these children are unable to meet normative affective and behavioral developmental demands. They begin development with an initial handicap that they carry on into childhood.

If problems first appear in middle childhood, they tend to be transient, within the time span studied. Few children who are free of problems in childhood develop problems in adolescence. The pathway of continual problems (at least three assessments) appears most often among the children of depressed mothers. Boys and girls are represented equally on the continual problem paths.

The pathway of continual problems may not be continuity of the same disorder. A given problem may subside, only to be followed by another kind of disturbance. Disruptive–oppositional problems succeed themselves more often in children of depressed mothers (27% to 33%) than in children of well mothers (7% to 10%). Trajectories of recurrent depressive problems especially single out the older children of depressed mothers (32% and 43% of children of bipolar and unipolar mothers, respectively). One child of a well mother has continual problems of depression. The individual pathways for anxiety are not highly different for children of well and depressed mothers.

EVOLUTION OF CHILDREN'S PATTERNS OF PROBLEMS

Further analyses take account of the child's *pattern* of problems, in order to observe developmental sequences in the patterns of problems. We begin with the *pattern* of problems that the child presents at a baseline and observe the evolution of the problems in the years following. The patterns are defined by the data: (1) depressed alone or with other internalizing, (2) depressed and externalizing, (3) anxious or somatic and externalizing, (4) anxious only, (5) somatic only, (6) externalizing only, and (7) no diagnosis (see Tables 7.3 and 7.4).

For the younger siblings, the baseline is the pattern of problems in the first 5 years. For these children, we focus on problem evolution through the prepubertal years (to 11 years). For the older

Table 7.1 *Longitudinal pathways of younger siblings, by mother's diagnosis (% of children)*

Psychiatric problem	Problem pathway	Mother's diagnosis			Pearson χ^2 df = 12
		Well	Bipolar	Unipolar	
Any problem	None	23.3	19.2	9.5	24.95, $p<.05$
	To age 6 only	36.7[a]	7.7	11.9	
	Before age 6 & recurs later	16.7	26.9	21.4	
	At ages 8 to 11 only	13.3	15.4	11.9	
	First at ages 8 to 11 & recurs later	3.3	3.9	0.0	
	First in adolescence	0.0	7.7	2.4	
	Continual problems	6.7[a]	19.2	42.9[a]	
Depressed	None	83.3[a]	57.7	38.1[a]	33.07, $p<.001$
	To age 6 only	0.0[a]	15.4	23.8[a]	
	Before age 6 & recurs later	3.3	0.0	11.9[a]	
	At ages 8 to 11 only	3.3	3.9	19.1[a]	
	First at ages 8 to 11 & recurs later	6.7	0.0	2.4	
	First in adolescence	3.3	15.4[a]	2.4	
	Continual problems	0.0	7.7	2.4	

Externalizing	None	66.7	53.9	40.5	22.06, $p<.05$
	To age 6 only	16.7	0.0^a	11.9	
	Before age 6 & recurs later	6.7	15.4	4.8	
	At ages 8 to 11 only	6.7	3.9	11.9	
	First at ages 8 to 11 & recurs later	3.3	0.0	2.4	
	First in adolescence	0.0^a	15.4^a	7.1	
	Continual problems	0.0^a	11.5	21.4^a	
Anxious	None	40.0	53.9^a	23.8	13.79, $p<.10$
	To age 6 only	36.7	11.5^a	26.2	
	Before age 6 & recurs later	10.0	11.5	28.6^a	
	At ages 8 to 11 only	13.3	23.1	19.1	
	First at ages 8 to 11 & recurs later	0.0	0.0	0.0	
	First in adolescence	0.0	0.0	0.0	
	Continual problems	0.0	0.0	2.4	

[a]Contribution of cell to $\chi^2 \geq 2.0$.

83

Table 7.2 *Longitudinal pathways of older siblings, by mother's diagnosis (% of children)*

Psychiatric problem	Problem pathway	Mother's diagnosis			Pearson χ^2 df = 12
		Well	Bipolar	Unipolar	
Any problem	None	30.0[a]	4.6	2.4[a]	30.95, $p<.005$
	At ages 5 to 7 only	6.7	4.6	4.8	
	At ages 5 to 7 & recurs later	16.7[a]	4.6	4.8	
	At ages 8 to 11 only	13.3[a]	4.6	2.4	
	First at ages 8 to 11 & recurs later	3.3	13.6	16.7	
	First in adolescence	10.0	18.2	7.1	
	Continual problems	20.0[a]	50.0	61.9[a]	
Depressed	None	63.3[a]	27.3	23.8[a]	24.68, $p<.05$
	At ages 5 to 7 only	10.0	4.6	4.8	
	At ages 5 to 7 & recurs later	0.0	0.0	9.5[a]	
	At ages 8 to 11 only	6.7	9.1	14.3	
	First at ages 8 to 11 & recurs later	0.0[a]	13.6	9.5	
	First in adolescence	16.7	27.3	14.3	
	Continual problems	3.3[a]	18.2	23.8	

Externalizing	None	80.0^a	50.0	28.6^a	30.54, $p<.005$
	At ages 5 to 7 only	3.3	4.6	7.1	
	At ages 5 to 7 & recurs later	3.3	4.6	9.5	
	At ages 8 to 11 only	0.0^a	0.0	16.7^a	
	First at ages 8 to 11 & recurs later	0.0	0.0	11.9^a	
	First in adolescence	10.0	18.2	14.3	
	Continual problems	3.3	22.7^a	11.9	
Anxious	None	56.7^a	36.4	21.4^a	19.46, $p<.08$
	At ages 5 to 7 only	3.3	4.6	14.3	
	At ages 5 to 7 & recurs later	10.0	0.0	7.1	
	At ages 8 to 11 only	16.7	13.6	14.3	
	First at ages 8 to 11 & recurs later	3.3	18.2^a	7.1	
	First in adolescence	10.0^a	22.7	31.0	
	Continual problems	0.0	4.6	4.8	

^{a}Contribution of cell to $\chi^2 \geq 2.0$.

Table 7.3 *Evolution of children's problems from the first 5 years to later prepubertal years (% of children)*[a]

Problems in the first 5 years	n	Problem in the prepubertal years						
		D	D+E	I+E	A	S	E	No Dx
Children of depressed mothers								
Depressed alone or with other internalizing (D)	1				100			
Depressed and externalizing (D+E)	2		50	50				
Anxious or somatic problems and externalizing (I+E)	4	50	25				25	
Anxious only (A)	11	18			18	36	9	18
Somatic problems only (S)	0							
Externalizing (E)	11		91			9		
No diagnosis (No Dx)	39	13	23	5	15	10	3	31
Children of well mothers								
D	0							
D+E	0							
I+E	2							100
A	7	14			14	14		57
S	0							
E	3				33	33		33
No Dx	18	11	6		28	11	6	39

[a]Col. 2 is the number of children with a given problem pattern in the first 5 years. Cols. 3–9 are the percentages of these children with a given pattern later on. Thus, 11 children (row 6) have early externalizing problems. Ten (91%) of these children (col. 4) are both depressed and externalizing in later prepubertal years.

Table 7.4 *Evolution of children's problems from the prepubertal years to the adolescent years (% of children)*[a]

Problems in the prepubertal years	n	Problem in adolescence						
		D	D+E	I+E	A	S	E	No Dx
Children of depressed mothers								
Depressed alone or with internalizing (D)	16	31	25	6	13	19	.	6
Depressed and externalizing (D+E)	20	15	50	10	5	10	5	5
Anxious or somatic problems and externalizing (I+E)	8	38	38	25	.	.	.	.
Anxious only (A)	4	.	25	.	50	.	.	25
Somatic problems only (S)	4	.	25	.	.	25	.	50
Externalizing only (E)	3	.	.	.	.	.	33	67
No diagnosis (No Dx)	9	33	11	11	11	.	11	22
Children of well mothers								
D	6	17	.	.	17	.	.	66
D+E	0	.	.	.	.	.	.	.
I+E	1	.	.	.	.	.	100	.
A	8	25	.	13	13	.	13	37
S	1	100	.	.	.	.	.	.
E	2	50	.	50	.	.	.	.
No Dx	12	.	8	.	8	8	.	75

[a]Col. 2 is the number of children with a given problem pattern in the prepubertal years (to 11 years). Cols. 3–9 are the percentages of these children with a given pattern in the adolescent years. Thus, 20 children have problems of depression in the prepubertal years (row 2), one (5%) is without a diagnosis (col. 9) in adolescence.

siblings, we have made the prepubertal years (5 to 11 years) the baseline and have followed the pattern of problems into adolescence. Column 1 in Tables 7.3 and 7.4 is the baseline pattern and column 2 is the number of children with this pattern. Columns 3–9 show the percentage of children of each baseline whose problems evolve in specified ways.

First 5 Years to Later Childhood

The evolution of initially disruptive problems of children of depressed mothers is especially striking. Seventeen preschoolers of depressed mothers had diagnoses of disruptive (externalizing) problems (see Table 7.3, rows 2, 3, and 6). Eleven were initially disruptive, without internalizing problems (row 6). However, over the prepubertal years, 10 of the 11 develop comorbid problems of depressive and disruptive problems. Children initially with comorbid patterns (rows 2 and 3) continue with comorbid problems or with depression or externalizing (6 out of 6). The 11 initially anxious children (row 4) tend to continue with internalizing problems (8 out of 11).

Problem patterns evolve differently in the children of well mothers. Many of their early problems disappear in childhood.

Childhood to Adolescence

The follow-up of problem patterns in the older siblings shifts the time frame – continuity or change from the prepubertal to the adolescent years (see Table 7.4). When depressive problems appear prior to 11 years, as they do in 56% of the older children of depressed mothers (see Table 7.4, rows 1 and 2), problems continue in 94% of the cases. Where the prepubertal pattern is depression alone (row 1), roughly two-thirds of these children are manifesting internalizing patterns in adolescence. Where disruptive disorders appear with depression in the prepubertal years (row 2), approximately two-thirds continue with comorbid problems in adolescence.

SUMMARY

Four points stand out in the evolution of problems:

1. Disruptive problems of preschool-age children of depressed mothers are rarely resolved and very often become comorbid with depression or other internalizing problems in childhood. Children of depressed mothers with depressive problems before 11 years continue to have problems in the adolescent period.

2. Maternal diagnosis is critical in predicting continuity in children's problems. Continuity of depression and disruptive problems is characteristic of the children of depressed mothers, but rarely so of the children of well mothers.

3. Internalizing problems are as continuous as externalizing problems in children of depressed mothers. Problems of children of well mothers are most often internalizing and usually remain internalizing or are resolved.

4. Looking back in time from adolescence, the offspring with adolescent diagnoses of comorbid internalizing and disruptive disorders rarely have had problem-free childhoods.

The path data emphasize the differences that underlie "outcome" classifications of children's psychopathology – differences in timing, pattern, sequence – any one of which may be important with regard to etiology and treatment. Preserving the identity of the individual child gives a sense of ongoing behavior, and retains the essential information of development in progress.

FROM DESCRIPTION OF CHILDREN'S PROBLEMS TO INVESTIGATIONS OF DETERMINANTS OF CHILDREN'S BEHAVIOR

In this and the preceding chapter, we have charted the emergence and evolution of children's disordered behavior. But these data do not provide information concerning the contexts in which the children are developing. Given only the broad frameworks of mother's diagnostic status and developmental stage, we have, at best, only hints of possible mechanisms influencing behavior.

Therefore, toward an understanding of factors contributing to children's maladaptive, as well as adaptive development, our investigation becomes a search for mechanisms of influence. Looking within mother's diagnosis and history, our first analyses, we are still many steps removed from identifying specific factors impacting on the child. Examinations, in later analyses, of specific qualities of family and mother more directly bring together processes in the individual and in the environment.

8

CHILDREN'S PROBLEMS IN RELATION TO CHARACTERISTICS OF MOTHER'S DEPRESSION AND ILLNESS HISTORY

Thus far the mother's diagnosis has been the single criterion for defining her depression and the only explanation offered for children's problems. However, no one assumes that all mothers within the diagnostic category are alike. Etiological differences in depression are expected, as are differences in the course of illness and in its impairing properties. Depressed mothers are not alike in the specific symptoms of their depression. Despite this heterogeneity, we have seen the integrity of the diagnosis as a carrier of risks for the offspring. Our purpose now is to determine whether and how the varied properties of mother's illness make a difference in the problems of the offspring.

We have examined five properties that have been reported in the literature as qualities of maternal depression associated with higher frequencies of offspring problems. These are properties pertaining to the background and course of the mother's depression, her level of functioning, and her personality disorders.

Each of these maternal variables is examined in relation to three "outcome" measures on the children: (1) a longitudinal measure of recurrent problems; (2) a diagnosis at ages 8 to 15 for the younger siblings, and at 11 to 19 for the older siblings; and (3) a summation of symptoms on the DICA (a child may have many and diverse symptoms but not reach criterion for a single diagnosis). The outcome assessment (T3,4) combines two evaluation periods.

91

When the child outcome variable is categorical (specific diagnoses), analyses are chi-squares for categorical predictor variables and t tests or Kruskal–Wallis for continuous or ranked variables, respectively. When the outcome variable is ordinal (recurrences), the analyses are Kendall's tau-b (concordant or discordant pairs with correction for ties) or logistic regression. For continuous outcome and predictor variables (symptom counts), the analyses are Pearson correlations, as well as regression analyses.

MOTHER'S AGE AT ONSET OF DEPRESSION

Early age of onset of depression is viewed in the literature as a possible indicator of genetic vulnerability and severity of the depression (Weissman, Wickramaratne, Merikangas, Leckman, Prushoff, Caruso, Kidd, & Gammon, 1984). One should expect, then, to find a relation between maternal age at onset and children's problems.

Mothers in our study varied in age at onset. The mean age at onset was 17.4 (SD = 8.5) for bipolar and 20.6 (SD = 9.5) for unipolar depressed mothers. Mother's age at onset of depression is not related to child's age at onset of depression. But, consistent with the findings of Weissman et al., early onset of depression in the mothers is significantly, but modestly, related to the DICA symptom count for the younger siblings (Pearson r = −.294, $p < .05$). Early onset of mother's depression is also a risk factor for recurrent disruptive problems in the younger siblings (tau-b = −.209, $p < .05$) and in the older siblings (tau-b = −.225, $p < .05$). The negative correlations indicate that earlier onset of mother's depression is associated with more problematic outcomes in the children.

FAMILY HISTORIES OF PSYCHIATRIC DISORDERS

Weissman, Gershon, Kidd, Prushoff, Leckman, Dibble, Hamovit, Thompson, Pauls, and Guroff (1984) have reported findings relating higher rates of depression in offspring to presence of psychiatric disorders, particularly affective disorders, among relatives. We interviewed mothers and fathers about psychiatric problems among their relatives (see chapter 4). Affective illness in one or more of their relatives was reported by 62% of the families with bipolar mothers and 44% of families with unipolar mothers, compared with only 17% of the families with well mothers. Families of unipolar, bipolar, and well mothers also differ significantly or at a trend level in the percent of first and second degree relatives having each type of psychiatric dysfunction. For every classification, the percent of relatives with disorders is lowest for well mothers, and highest for bipolar mothers.

Family history, however, within any maternal group, is not consistently related to children's problems. We suggest this is not surprising in light of the research design in which the parents' affective illness gives our children a common family background of affective illness.

MAJOR EPISODES OF MOTHER'S DEPRESSION

The severity and chronicity of mother's depression have been found to relate to increased offspring problems (Keller et al., 1986). Following this lead, we looked to two possible indices of severity of mother's depression: frequency of episodes and length of time in episodes. These two descriptors are not so readily transformed into solid measures, however. We abandoned number of episodes as a measure because the length of episodes varied greatly, giving questionable meaning to the count of episodes. A single episode reported by some mothers covered considerably more time than the combined time of multiple episodes of other mothers. Also, retrospective reporting further undermines faith in this measure. We used amount of time in episodes, also an approximation, and subject to retrospective error, as the maternal variable to relate to children's functioning.

The mean reported length of time in episodes was 496 (SD =

586) weeks for bipolar and 264 (SD = 398) weeks for unipolar mothers. (Scores were ranked and normalized for analysis because of substantial positive skewing.)

Amount of time in episodes is significantly related to the younger siblings' DICA symptom count (Pearson r = .235, $p <$ .05) and to the longitudinal measure of recurrence of disruptive problems (tau-b = .215, $p <$ .05) in the older siblings – a longer time in episodes is associated with more symptoms and more recurrent disruptive disorders. This association is open to alternative interpretations: Severity is indicative of genetic vulnerability; severity is also an environmental variable increasing the child's exposure to a functionally impaired mother.

MOTHER'S LEVEL OF FUNCTIONING (GAF)

We investigated another quality indicative of the severity of mother's depression, namely, the level of behavioral impairment (GAF score). It, too, is related to children's problems. A low GAF score (poor functioning) is predictive of child problems. Maternal GAF score is related to the younger children's DICA symptom count (Pearson r = $-.279$, $p <$ .05) and to recurrent disruptive problems (tau-b = $-.277$, $p <$ .01). Maternal GAF score is related to the older siblings' recurrent problems (tau-b = $-.208$, $p <$ .05).

MATERNAL PERSONALITY DISORDERS

Only occasionally have personality disorders been included in research on maternal depression and its effects on offspring. When they have been included, they have been found to add significantly to offspring risk (Rutter & Quinton, 1984). This finding is replicated in the present study.

Many of the depressed mothers have personality disorders (diagnostic interview, chapter 4). Some 67% of the mothers with bipolar illness, 54% of the mothers with unipolar depression, and 19% of the well mothers were diagnosed with at least one per-

94

Table 8.1 *Percentage of mothers with personality disorders*

	Mother's diagnosis		
Personality disorder	Well ($n = 27$)	Bipolar ($n = 24$)	Unipolar ($n = 41$)
Paranoid	0	8	7
Schizoid	0	4	2
Schizotypal	0	17	2
Histrionic	7	21	12
Narcissistic	0	4	5
Antisocial	0	4	7
Borderline	0	38	20
Sadistic	0	4	5
Avoidant	0	21	15
Dependent	4	13	7
Obsessive–compulsive	7	8	10
Passive–aggressive	0	13	5
Self-defeating	0	0	7
Any disorder	19	67	54
Multiple disorders	0	46	24

Source: Adapted from DeMulder, Tarullo, Klimes-Dougan, Free, and Radke-Yarrow, 1995.

sonality disorder (χ^2 (2) = 13.3, $p < .001$) (Table 8.1). When mothers are evaluated on a dimensional score on personality disorders, bipolar and unipolar mothers have significantly higher symptom scores than well mothers (F(2,89) = 29.45, $p<.0001$).

Personality disorders in depressed mothers have significance for children's functioning: High scores on disorders predict child problems. For the younger siblings, dimensional scores are correlated with symptom counts (Pearson r = .318, $p < .01$), and are related to the presence of disruptive problems ($t(66)$ = 2.00, $p < .05$), and "any" problem ($t(66)$ = 2.85, $p < .01$). For the older siblings, mother's dimensional scores are related to recurrent problematic disruptive behavior and recurrent "any" problems (tau-b = .243, $p < .01$, and tau-b = .192, $p < .05$, respectively).

Measured as present or not, personality disorder is associated with a diagnosis of depression (19.5% of children of mothers without and 42.1% of children of mothers with a personality disorder, respectively, $\chi^2(1) = 4.02, p < .05$).

Of the multiple personality disorders occurring in the depressed mothers, avoidant, dependent, and borderline are the most common. We examined associations between these disorders and specific child problems, finding few specific associations. The exceptions are links between avoidant and dependent personality disorders in the mother and disruptive disorders in the child. Repeated disruptive diagnoses appear in 55% of older children with an avoidant mother, and in 7% and 0% of children without or with probable avoidant disorder, respectively ($\chi^2(6) = 19.03, p < .01$). Repeated disruptive disorders appear in 50% of younger children of mothers with a dependent disorder (in 0% without a disorder and 17% with a probable disorder, $\chi^2(6) = 12.65, p < .05$).

To speculate, one would expect avoidant personality to translate into unavailable or uninvolved mothering, and dependent personality into overinvolvement. Maternal personality disorders, perhaps through these mechanisms, significantly increase children's disruptive behavior.

QUALITIES OF MOTHER'S ILLNESS MOST PREDICTIVE OF SPECIFIC CHILD OUTCOMES

From a review of our findings on the effects of mother's illness qualities on child problems, we see that disruptive problems in the offspring and summary measures that include diverse problems are quite consistently predicted by the maternal variables. We find, too, that the five qualities of maternal illness are highly interrelated (see Table 8.2). Nine of 10 correlations are significant in the predicted direction (alpha = .05); seven are significant with Bonferoni adjustment for multiple comparisons (.005). Because of the correlations among the variables, we decided to search for the best predictors of those child outcome variables that were most

Table 8.2 *Pearson correlations (p) among qualifiers of mother's illness*

	Age at onset	GAF score	Time in episodes	PDE score
GAF	.38 (<.001)			
Time in episodes	−.68 (<.001)	−.47 (<.001)		
PDE score	−.44 (<.001)	−.68 (<.001)	.40 (<.001)	
Family history	−.35 (<.005)	−.08	.26 (<.05)	.26 (<.05)

often predicted by the single mother qualities; namely, symptom counts and recurrent disruptive problems.

Logistic regression was used when recurrent disruptive disorder was the outcome; linear multiple regression, when the number of symptoms was the outcome. (Only the younger siblings are involved in symptom counts, because no maternal variables predicted symptom counts in the older cohort.) Five predictor variables (illness qualities) are included in each regression: For the younger siblings, the mother's score on personality disorders is the strongest predictor of DICA symptom counts ($F(1,66) = 7.45$, $p < .01$, $R^2 = .10$), and mother's age at onset of depression is the strongest predictor of recurrent or continual disruption ($\chi^2(1) = 3.72$, $p = .05$). For the older siblings, the mother's GAF score is the most significant predictor of recurrent disruptive disorders ($\chi^2(1) = 7.81$, $p < .01$).

SUMMARY

Each of the qualities of mother's depression that has tapped a dimension of severity of depression or reduced functional adequacy of the mother is related, in some manner, to increased risk for the children. Although each quality, individually, shows some relation to child problems, the mother with a high score on personality disorders is likely to have a low GAF score, early age of onset, more time in episodes, and more family history. The qualities do not, therefore, make independent contributions to child outcome. We have not learned much from these associations regarding mechanisms through which these variables have their influence. We will reexamine some of these maternal qualities in combination with family variables and mother–child relationships (chapters 10 and 12).

9

FAMILY ENVIRONMENTS: CASE DESCRIPTIONS

> A necessary consequence of the family's complexity is
> that each characteristic of the family and each type of
> experience that a child may have within the family (i.e.,
> each independent variable) may be related to many out-
> come measures (i.e., dependent variables), and each de-
> pendent variable to many independent ones.
> R. A. Hinde (1980, p. 47)

The complexity of family environments is apparent in research
on parental depression. Family dysfunction and stresses are frequent, and difficulties for the children are inevitable. Stresses and
strengths in the family are not readily measurable, except in
broad, almost obvious dimensions that do not specifically identify how they involve and affect individual children. The complexity of family experiences and their potential influences are
illustrated in two families in which there are multiple painful experiences.

FAMILY B

This middle-class family with six children lives in the suburbs in
a small three-bedroom house that shows the wear and tear of use.
There is little space for anyone to be alone. Finances are tight. The
children complain about wearing second-hand clothes. They also
"get on each other's nerves."

Janet and Morna, the children in the study, are fourth and fifth
in birth order. Preceding them are Lisa, the oldest, Edgar, and Joe,
and following them is Maureen. Lisa and Edgar have made such

a strong imprint on the life of this family that Janet and Morna are almost invisible.

Mrs. B has a long history of depression. When Janet was 6 years old, Mrs. B's depression was severe – for 6 months she could "barely get through the day." She relied heavily on Lisa for help with the laundry and child care. Mrs. B. was also very depressed during and after her last pregnancy. She couldn't sleep. She lost 50 pounds. She had thoughts of suicide. She describes herself: "I wasn't really there." "I dimly remember nursing Maureen, but I couldn't even talk to her."

Mrs. B was exhausted. Laundry piled up; dishes got stacked; the groceries weren't bought. Lisa was no longer willing to take on these responsibilities. Things just didn't get done.

Mr. B was no support. He didn't help around the house; he didn't help with the care of the children. When he came home from work, he wanted dinner on the table and his liter of beer. After dinner, he'd doze off in front of the TV. It took the family a long time to realize that Mr. B was drinking excessively and often was only vaguely aware of what was going on in the family. He had a bad accident cutting the lawn. He cut off the tips of his fingers with the lawn mower and was in agony for weeks.

Mrs. B was used to accidents in the family. Lisa broke her collarbone twice in elementary school. Edgar broke his leg, and later broke both wrists falling off his bike. In one of the free-for-alls, Edgar threw a rocky mud ball at Janet, which made a large cut in her forehead, resulting in a trip to the hospital. This pattern of breaks and blood and Lisa's perennial episodes of headaches and stomachaches left Mrs. B generally unresponsive to the children's complaints of pain. When Lisa was 10 years old, an appendicitis attack went unheeded for several days because her mother discounted Lisa's whining as just "more of the same." Five years later, Lisa's physical pain was again ignored, only for Lisa to end up in the hospital for an operation for kidney stones.

Lisa was now 15. Her behavior was deteriorating in many ways. She was doing poorly in school. She stayed away from home. She lied about her whereabouts. She would erupt in terrible anger when she was at home. Only now she told her parents that she had been raped five years earlier by the boys for whom Mrs. B was providing temporary foster care. (Janet, too, had been molested.)

Lisa, according to her mother, became a "daredevil." For example, she joined a dance contest and danced so long and frantically that she could hardly walk. For relief, she went for a swim but dived in the wrong end of the pool and broke her nose.

Eventually Lisa turned her anger on her parents. She reported dreaming that she had used an axe on them (and she brought an axe from the basement and kept it in her room). Even Mr. B was aroused to action. Hospitalization was arranged. Mrs. B reported, "For the family, this is a terrific relief. Everybody is safe, she's safe, we're safe. We are beginning to laugh around the dinner table. We can talk to one another."

It was not enough that Mrs. B's energies were fully taken with Lisa's problems. All of the time she was also dealing with Edgar, who had severe learning difficulties. She had to help him constantly with his homework. He was easily frustrated and would break things and pound on his brother when he was angry. He was big, and the other children were afraid of him and tried to stay out of his way. He began to hear voices, which made him fiercely angry. After a particularly violent episode, Mr. B took Edgar forcibly to the hospital. After some months in the hospital, he was placed in a halfway house. This frightened Janet, who feared an encounter with him, should he make a surprise visit home. "I feel I have grown up looking over my shoulder wondering what will happen next." Mrs. B added to the reality of this fear by bringing Edgar along on a family picnic – at which he became predictably violent.

Lisa was now out of the hospital. She came home, rebellious and angry, verbally abusive, totally uncontrollable. After enduring for several months, Mr. B kicked Lisa out of the house. Mrs. B still focused on Lisa's "good points," but it was no longer possible to deny her problems when Lisa got involved in drugs and arrived back home announcing that she was pregnant. This was difficult for this religiously devout family. They did not want an abortion.

101

They turned to the church for counsel. This led to a dividend, the first in this family's turbulent history. Through the services of the church, they got into a family counseling service, and the beginnings of support were established. Mr. B accepted counseling and help for his drinking. Lisa's pregnancy, which involved repeated emergency trips to the hospital, for the first time brought the family together. The tensions, for the time at least, had somewhat subsided. Janet, reflecting on her family, wondered if her "poor colorful family" was the only one to have so many problems.

FAMILY H

Mrs. H is very depressed and has been depressed for much of her adult life. She has been characteristically whiny and complaining each time she is seen at the research laboratory.

Her husband did not know of her depression when they got married. They had an exciting common goal; they were building a house for themselves in a lovely wooded area. Mr. H threw himself wholeheartedly into the building project and they lived in parts of the house as it was being built.

Annie, a wanted child, was born in this period. But the promise that the house and the baby held faded rapidly. The fact that Mrs. H's husband's family lived nearby and strongly favored him over her added to her blue moods.

Mrs. H's depression grew worse. She stayed in bed much of the time. Annie was her one comfort. Mrs. H described her love and affection for Annie; they were almost like one and were together constantly. When Mark was born, Annie had an unusually strong reaction. He was an unwelcome intruder between her and her mother. Mrs. H's mother was a big help, especially when Mrs. H was unable to function.

Marital tensions grew. Mr. and Mrs. H fought over the house until they sold it and moved to a townhouse ten miles away. This turned out to be no comfort to Mrs. H. "Everything that could go wrong did go wrong." Mrs. H remembered that her bouts with depression began at a time in her life when her family also had moved. Annie hadn't wanted to move. Mrs. H worried about Annie, who might, she thought, be experiencing the same depressed feelings. Mrs. H described herself as being just like Annie – "quiet, cooperative, and very close to my mother."

When the family came to the research apartment, Annie was 7 and Mark was 2. Mark looked rumpled and dirty. Mrs. H sheepishly confided that, when she was as tired as she had been recently, she didn't have the energy to give him a bath. Annie was fresh and clean and very carefully groomed. During the morning, she admired herself in the mirrors and carefully brushed her long hair. Mark brought a high level of energy. He moved impulsively and seemed confined in the space. A research procedure that required a delay of gratification was more aggravating to him than to most children his age. His mother just shrugged and returned to listlessly watching TV "soaps."

Annie had recently become ill and was diagnosed with juvenile diabetes. Her mother could be of no help to her. The mother's mother had to be called to help Annie learn to give her own insulin shots. Mr. H was of no help. He denied the seriousness of Annie's illness, but then he came to realize that he would have to keep his job (one he found frustrating) just to maintain his current health insurance.

By the end of the morning in the apartment, Mark had the toys scattered everywhere. Mrs. H sighed as she looked helplessly at the chaos. "This is what my house looks like all of the time, and I just can't deal with it."

At the second assessment, the father accompanied the family. He and Mark were fully engaged in building a fantastic tower. Annie seemed to be trying to pull her mother out of her depression and to bring her parents into some positive interaction. She enacted an elaborate restaurant game around lunch, but she very pointedly left her "pesky brother" out of it.

In the psychiatric interview, Annie kept tight control of her feelings, but acknowledged a few worries and feeling like running away when her mother seemed to take Mark's side. She became agitated when questioned about her parents and gave brief nods as answers and did not want to talk about her own health.

103

At home, Annie and Mark took care of themselves, in a fashion. There were many children in the townhouse complex, and Mark invested in them. He played vigorously in the common yard supplied with play equipment.

Mr. H spent less and less time with his family. He took a night job. This gave him some time during the day, which he spent with his son. He wanted his son to do well in school. He was angry with his wife for allowing Mark to stay home from school. If Mark didn't want to go, he was allowed to stay home. He watched TV and his mother stayed in bed. She was totally centered on her own problems and feelings. She felt that she was a failure. She gained a lot of weight and developed a troubled rash that marred her face.

The closeness between mother and Annie that so characterized infancy and early childhood was long gone. Annie showed little caring or empathy when her mother was depressed.

Mother and father fought a lot. Annie would side with her father. Finally Mr. H moved out. Annie (age 13) was so angry she moved to live with her paternal grandmother – in a house in the woods. She soon gained her grandmother's perspective regarding her mother.

10

FAMILY ENVIRONMENTS OF DEPRESSION

The children of depressed and well mothers have grown up (or nearly so) in our descriptions of their functioning. Up to this point in our analyses, we have observed their problems but have asked little about the behavioral contexts in which their problems have developed. The children and their mothers have been viewed mainly as "vehicles of psychopathology" (Rutter & Shaffer, 1980). We now turn to experiences in the children's lives, to investigate associations between these experiences and their problems, and to search for mechanisms that foster or protect against maladaptive development. In this chapter, we investigate characteristics of the children's families. In following chapters, there is a finer focus on mother–child relationships. Then we turn to characteristics of the child as a variable interacting with family variables and the mother–child relationship. Together these three contextual foci provide detailed and discriminating measures of the child's environment. As avenues of influence they are clearly not independent of one another.

MEASURING FAMILY STRESS

Families with an affectively ill parent member have repeatedly been found to live under adverse conditions of chronic stresses and traumatic events. This co-occurrence of parental depression and family stress has been variously interpreted. From one perspective, depressive symptoms and family stressors are inseparable expressions of the illness. From another perspective, life events and conditions are regarded as precipitating factors in mother's depression. In a purely genetic explanation of depression, environmental variables are etiologically irrelevant. In still another model, the interacting factors of illness and environment are considered.

Investigations of family stress as an influence on the offspring of depressed parents have generally involved the variables common to studies of other high-risk groups, namely, marital discord, conflicts among other family members, health problems, financial matters, and personal losses. We have followed the field, interviewing the mother concerning family functioning in these areas.

Data on the general family milieu are essential ground-level information about the child's environments, although limited in explanatory power. Although the research question concerning family stress has the sound of tidiness (how does family stress contribute to child outcomes?) stress represents a complex set of conditions. Multiple stresses, interrelatedness of stresses, and variable timing of traumatic events and conditions are but some of the complexities involved in attempting to relate family stress to offspring development.

A further difficulty lies in the fact that the familiar variables of stress are broadly defined with reference to the family, and imperfectly assess the stress for the individual child. For example, consider marital discord, a much emphasized variable in research on depression. Marital discord can enter into children's lives in very different ways (Engfer, 1988). Children may be exposed to parents' frightening fighting, to a parent's threat of, or actual leaving, to anger vented on them. The strains on the child will vary: fear of physical harm, fear of loss of parent, self-blame, and so on.

Against this background of complexity, we used ratings of stress in each of the areas of family functioning, at successive assessment periods (see chapter 4 for procedures). We scored stress in a number of ways. In addition to specific area ratings, we created composite scores, based on Factor Analyses, at each time period. At T1 and T2, the stresses all loaded highly on a single Factor. We used the mean of the five areas of stress to represent total stress at each period. At T3, two Factors emerged, one based largely on marital discord, family conflicts, and housing and money stress (labeled interpersonal stress), the other based on health problems and loss (labeled health/loss stress). These two Factors also are represented by means of the high loading variables. Cumulative stress over time is the mean of each stress over the three time periods.

We have compared the family environments of children of depressed and well mothers. Then, separately for depressed and well groups, we have examined associations between family stress and offspring functioning. Preliminary analyses showed that combining the groups results in spurious findings relating to stress, which, in fact, could be explained by mother's diagnosis alone.

STRESS IN FAMILIES OF DEPRESSED AND WELL MOTHERS

What is the texture of life in families of depressed and well mothers? The findings are not unexpected. The mean family-wide stress level in each area of stress differs significantly ($p < .05$) by maternal diagnosis, at each developmental time period, except with regard to health at the T3 assessment. The lowest mean stress is always in the well families. Bipolar and unipolar mother groups differ only for marital stress in the early childhood period, with more stress in the bipolar families ($\chi^2(1) = 6.68$, $p < .01$). The family environments, expressed as percentages of families with high levels of stress (see Table 10.1), show the marked group differences.

Psychiatric illness in the father in the families of depressed mothers contributes to level of stress. These families suffer more stress than families with a well father, at each time period (all $p < .01$).

Differences between families of depressed and well mothers are not only in "degree" of stress. Correlations of stress levels from one time period to the next are stronger in the families of depressed than of well mothers, especially in marital discord and discord over housing and money matters (see Table 10.2). In other words, stresses are more continuous in families with depressed mothers than in families of well parents.

Table 10.1 *Percentage of families with high stress, by mother's diagnosis and time of assessment*

		Areas of stress					
Mother's diagnosis	Time of assessment	Marital discord	Other family conflict	Housing and money matters	Loss of significant persons	Health problems
Well	T1	6.7	0.0	10.0	6.7	40.0
	T2	10.0	6.7	6.7	10.0	40.0
	T3	13.3	10.0	3.3	30.0	46.7
Bipolar depressed	T1	76.0	28.0	40.0	32.0	80.0
	T2	76.0	36.0	28.0	40.0	84.0
	T3	61.5	38.5	30.8	57.7	57.7
Unipolar depressed	T1	53.7	34.2	36.6	24.4	63.4
	T2	58.5	31.7	29.3	26.8	58.5
	T3	52.5	39.0	29.3	53.7	65.9

Table 10.2 *Kendall tau-b correlations (p) of stress levels over time, in families of well and depressed mothers*

Mother's diagnosis	Time of assessment		Areas of stress			
		Marital discord	Other family conflict	Housing and money matters	Loss of significant persons	Health problems
Well	T1 with T2	.79 (<.0001)	.46 (<.01)	.65 (<.0001)	.09	.51 (<.001)
	T1 with T3	.16	.08	.16	.10	.21
	T2 with T3	.06	.12	.35 (<.05)	.05	.32 (<.05)
Depressed	T1 with T2	.79 (<.0001)	.73 (<.0001)	.57 (<.0001)	.12	.44 (<.0001)
	T1 with T3	.32 (<.01)	.06	.39 (<.001)	.18	.05
	T2 with T3	.39 (<.001)	.14	.41 (<.0001)	.17	.12

An important difference between families of well and depressed mothers that is not reflected in the stress ratings appears in the correlations among stressors. The various areas of stress are not interrelated in the well families, but they are interrelated in the families of depressed mothers (see Table 10.3). Marital discord is significantly correlated with each of the other areas of stress. Because this is not the case in families of well mothers, we cannot legitimately compare influences of marital discord on offspring in depressed and well families. Marital stress in depressed families carries with it an abundance of other stresses that may affect the child.

Then, too, qualitative differences in the stresses enter into comparisons of family conditions and their influences on children in high- and low-risk families. Not only is there extensive compounding and chronicity in stresses in the families of depressed mothers, but the kinds of co-occurring problems often seem out of the ordinary. While ratings of high stress in the well families are likely to be for illness, loss of job, problems of housing, husband–wife arguments, and the like, in the highly stressed families of depressed mothers, parents yell and fight physically, father throws the family out of the house, the older sibling threatens mother with a knife, the father gives mother no money for household needs, the child is sexually abused by a live-in relative. The experiences to which children are exposed are so different qualitatively that comparison by the usual quantitative yardstick does not do justice to the phenomena.

In families of depressed mothers, stress is further qualitatively distinct by virtue of the strains introduced by behavioral impairments in the mother that are inherent in her illness. We find that mother's symptomatically impaired functioning at the time of entry into the study (GAS) is significantly associated with marital discord, other family conflicts, and total family stress (tau-b = $-.30$, tau-b = $-.26$, tau-b = $-.25$, respectively, all $p < .01$). This combination of maternal impairments with other family stresses imposes a critical mass of strains at a critical early time in the child's development, when basic patterns of behavior and perception are being established. At the end of childhood (T3), again a

Table 10.3 *Kendall tau-b correlations (p) between stresses at each time period, in families of depressed and well mothers*

Correlated stresses	Depressed mothers			Well mothers		
	Time 1	Time 2	Time 3	Time 1	Time 2	Time 3
Marital relationships						
with nonspousal conflicts	.36 (<.001)	.33 (<.001)	.14	.26	.06	.03
with housing/money	.36 (<.001)	.22 (<.05)	.32 (<.01)	.23	−.02	.11
with loss of significant person	.38 (<.001)	.30 (<.01)	.36 (<.001)	.02	.22	.39 (<.01)
with health	.23 (<.05)	−.05	−.19	−.02	−.17	−.04
Nonspousal conflicts						
with housing money	.23 (<.05)	.40 (<.001)	.23 (<.05)	.05	.11	−.04
with loss of significant person	.15	.32 (<.01)	.08	−.02	−.28	.05
with health	.10	.30 (<.01)	.01	−.18	−.19	.04
Housing/money						
with loss of significant person	.22 (<.05)	.23 (<.05)	.14	.25	.43 (<.01)	.02
with health	.07	.15	−.14	−.10	−.03	.30
Loss of significant persons						
with health	.32 (<.01)	.12	.15	.11	.19	.20

critical transitional period in development, mother's impairments, in this instance, her personality disorders, are associated with dimensions of family stress: marital discord, housing and money problems, and interpersonal stress (tau-b = .19, tau-b = .22, tau-b = .21, respectively, all $p < .05$).

A conceptual complication becomes apparent: The mother's depression-impaired behavior, a stressor in the life of the family, is correlated with other stresses and may be a significant contributor to some of them. But the mother's impaired behavior also defines her diagnosis of depression. The conceptual independence or separation of maternal diagnosis and family stress is blurred. What, then, can be concluded concerning the relative contributions of diagnosis and stress from this level of data?

STRESS IN FAMILIES OF DEPRESSED MOTHERS IN RELATION TO CHILDREN'S PSYCHIATRIC PROBLEMS

As an index of the child's maladaptive behavior we used the number of symptoms on the DICA at the end of childhood. To look for relations between children's problems and stress at each time period or cumulative stress we used stepwise linear regression.

Interpersonal family stress measured at T3 emerged as a modest but consistent predictor of offspring symptoms. Total number of symptoms, number of internalizing symptoms, and number of externalizing symptoms in the younger siblings are related to interpersonal stress ($F(1,62) = 12.11$, $R^2 = .16$; $F(1,62) = 11.92$, $R^2 = .16$; $F(1,62) = 8.15$, $R^2 = .12$, respectively, all $p < .01$). Total number of symptoms and number of internalizing symptoms in the older siblings are related to interpersonal stress ($F(1,58) = 4.53$, $p < .05$, $R^2 = .07$; $F(1,58) = 7.70$, $p < .01$, $R^2 = .12$, respectively). On this very general summary measure, level of family stress and offspring problems are related.

The consistency in associations between stress and child problems quickly breaks down when specific offspring problems or specific areas of stress are considered. Only scattered associations appear: Depression is significantly associated with stress in only two of many comparisons: Younger siblings' depression at T3,4 is related to housing and money stress at T3 ($\chi^2(1) = 4.38, p < .05$), and older siblings' depression at T1 is associated with loss at that time ($\chi^2(1) = 3.96, p < .05$). Only younger siblings' disruptive problems at T3 are related to cumulative family conflict ($t(65) = 3.25, p < .01$). Younger siblings' anxiety at T2 is related to housing and money stress at that time ($\chi^2(1) = 5.11, p < .05$). Older siblings' anxiety at T3 is related to cumulative family conflict ($t(61) = 2.74, p < .01$). As these few findings demonstrate, associations between family stress and offspring functioning are not compelling.

There is a further difficulty in interpreting the findings on stress effects. While theoretically the developmental timing of stress is an important consideration, chronic stress in most of these families gives little opportunity to tease out specific stress effects in relation to specific developmental periods.

In a further analysis, we used as a measure of stress the combination of family stress ratings (high or low) at T3 and ratings (high or low) of the mother's impaired functioning. We reasoned that we are closer to the child's experience by including in family stress the difficulties that are generated by the mother's symptoms of depression. We grouped families on the combined sources of stress, thereby arriving at the presumed highest level of stressors, intermediate levels, and lowest level. Children's problems associated with these patterns are shown in Table 10.4.

The combined sources of high stress do not provide additional prediction of psychiatric problems in the preadolescent children, but they have an impressive effect on the older siblings. The highest rates of depression (67%) are associated with the combination of mother's impairment (low GAF) and high family stress (an association not found in the separate analyses of these stressors). With unimpaired functioning and low family stress, 26% of the children have depressive problems. With unimpaired mothers and high interpersonal stress, or with impaired mothers and low family stress, rates of children's problems are intermediate (Mantel-Haenszel $\chi^2 = 4.86, p < .05$). The combinations of Health/Loss

Table 10.4 *Current family stress and mother's impaired functioning (GAF) and personality disorder (PD) in relation to children's problems (% of children)*

Family stress and mother's impairment	Problems in younger siblings, 8–11 years				Problems in older siblings, 11–15 years			
	n	Depressed	Anxious	External-izing	n	Depressed	Anxious	External-izing
Interpersonal stress and mother's GAF								
Normal GAF/low stress	28	14.3	39.3	28.6	27	25.9	40.7	11.1
Low GAF/low stress or normal GAF/high stress	30	30.0	46.7	26.7	28	42.9	42.9	39.3
Low GAF/high stress	10	20.0	50.0	60.0	9	66.7 ($p<.05$)	66.7	33.3 ($p<.05$)
Health/loss stress and mother's GAF								
Normal GAF/low stress	18	27.8	38.9	38.9	18	27.8	44.4	33.3
Low GAF/low stress or normal GAF/high stress	37	21.6	46.0	24.3	35	34.3	45.7	14.3
Low GAF/high stress	13	15.4	46.2	46.2	11	72.7 ($p<.05$)	45.5	54.6

Interpersonal stress and mother's PD								
No PD/low stress	20	5.0	30.0	10.0	18	22.2	44.4	5.6
PD/low stress or no PD/high stress	24	28.8	50.0	45.8	23	34.8	39.1	30.4
PD/high stress	23	34.8	52.2	39.1	22	59.1	50.0	40.9
		$(p<.05)$		$(p<.05)$		$(p<.01)$		$(p<.01)$
Health/loss stress and mother's PD								
No PD/low stress	12	16.7	25.0	16.7	12	8.3	33.3	16.7
PD/low stress or no PD/high stress	27	14.8	48.2	37.0	24	41.7	62.5	20.8
PD/high stress	28	28.6	50.0	35.7	27	51.9	33.3	37.0
				$(p<.05)$				

stress and maternal impairment follow a similar pattern. The findings are also similar for the joint influences of maternal personality disorders and interpersonal family stress or with health/loss stress (all $p < .05$).

Although the findings are clear, the interpretation is less so. Mother's behavior is both a stressor and an index of the severity of her depression. As observed earlier, effects of mother's diagnosis and family stress are not easily disentangled.

STRESS IN FAMILIES OF DEPRESSED MOTHERS IN RELATION TO CHILDREN'S DAY-TO-DAY FUNCTIONING

In further search of the influences of stress on children of depressed mothers, we examined children's day-to-day functioning. Interestingly, there are more specific associations and more consistent associations between family stress and children's daily functioning than between stress ratings and children's diagnoses. Poor peer relationships and less favorable self-concept are associated with high health/loss stress (peer relationships of the younger children with health/loss stress and with cumulative health stress, tau-b $= -.20$, p $< .05$, tau-b $= -.26$, $p < .01$, respectively; self-concept of the older siblings with health/loss stress, tau-b $= -.27$, $p < .05$). Family turmoil has damaging influences on the school performance of children of depressed mothers. Poor school performance by the younger children is associated with cumulative family conflict (tau-b $= -.24$) and with cumulative health stress (tau-b $= -.25$; all $p < .05$). Poor school performance by the older siblings is associated with cumulative marital stress (tau-b $= -.27$. $p < .01$) and cumulative housing and money stress (tau-b $= -.24$, $p < .05$).

Conclusions regarding the effects of stress in families of depressed parents are difficult to make. We will come back to this question after first examining the influences of family stress on children in well families.

STRESS IN FAMILIES OF WELL MOTHERS IN RELATION TO CHILDREN'S PROBLEMS

As already noted, stressful family conditions are not a way of life for most children in well families. When stressors occur or develop, they tend to be neither chronic nor embedded in a host of family problems. It is possible, therefore, to see the family and child before, during, and after the identified stressor event or condition.

The low rates of stress give us limited variation in the well families. We find associations, only at trend levels ($p < .06$ to $.09$), between health and financial stresses in the preschool and early school years and children's problems appearing at the same time period. Also, at T3 assessment, financial stress and children's disruptive problems are related ($p < .08$). The data suggest that specific stressors trigger children's problems, which are tied, in time, to the presence of the stress.

An interesting counterintuitive association appears between family stress and children's self-concepts that is consistent with this suggestion. In the older children of well parents, those with the most positive self-concepts come from families with high health/loss stress, and high cumulative health stress (tau-b = $.31$, tau-b = $.37$, both $p < .05$). Inspection of the family conditions indicated that a number of well families were confronted with serious health threats. In the face of these threats, these families were mobilized into warm family cohesiveness, in which case a positive self-concept is in keeping with the family response to stress.

A telling difference between well and depressed families is in regard to family stress and children's school performance. While performance suffered in the children of depressed parents, in well families, school performance is not significantly affected by family stresses.

But all is not well in our well families. Some are visited by adversity, and some few children ($n = 9$) have had very troubled development, characterized by disruptive and depressive disorders. Examination of the family conditions in the lives of these

117

children links family adversity and children with problems. Several themes emerge. Seven of the children have experienced multiple or repeated losses or threats of losses (e.g., losing a parent or affectively close grandparent, being uprooted, losing friends, serious illness of parent, losing a positive relationship with a parent). In the families of five of the seven children, there is also marital discord.

There is, however, a positive note to these stressed families and troubled children: All of the children are functioning well or excelling in academic or artistic or athletic performance. Their investment in achievement (probably with support from the parents) appears to be a strong and sustaining factor in their survival.

PROTECTIVE FACTORS IN THE ENVIRONMENTS OF CHILDREN OF DEPRESSED MOTHERS

To evaluate family environments of children solely on dimensions of stress is an incomplete assessment. Garmezy (1985) and Rutter (1985), among other investigators, have brought attention to protective factors that can moderate the impact of stressors. Supportive relationships, a fortunate change in circumstances (e.g., moving out of a bad neighborhood), and special qualities of the individual offspring have been noted as having protective potential.

Not surprisingly, we found that supportive persons make a difference in offspring functioning. We compared children who are without diagnoses at T3,4, children with diagnoses but functioning well, and children with diagnoses and functioning poorly in relation to the supports available to them. They differ overwhelmingly. Depressed mothers were rated supportive of 73% and 65% of the younger and older siblings, respectively, who have no diagnosis; of 56% and 36% of the children with a diagnosis but functioning well; and of only 17% and 17% of the children with a diagnosis and functioning poorly. Support from siblings and

118

peers, as reported by the child (Family and Friends, see chapter 4), shows a similar picture. Fathers' support has directionally similar effects.

Although it is reasonable to conclude that these supports have beneficial effects on the children, it is also possible that the child's level of functioning differently draws support from others. The data cannot make this directional distinction, hence we may be observing both protective and response roles of the family members.

COMMENTS ON STRESS

That conditions and relationships in families with a depressed parent are often stressful is clear. That the consequences of these conditions on the children can best be investigated with the general concept of "stress" is less clear. Research has arrived at a kind of plateau in explaining precisely what, how, and when family stress variables affect offspring development.

By aggregating diverse family stresses into quantitative stress indices, the possibility of examining the qualitative configurations is lost. By formulating the process as one of stress effects on offspring, the offspring become passive recipients of risks, although it is quite evident that they are differently receptive and responsive. By only minimally capturing the sequential over time connectedness of the stressful conditions and relationships, a significant aspect of process is missed. The phenomenon of stressful environment needs better definition and longitudinal measurement.

The distinguishing characteristics of families of depressed mothers – multiple and over-time repeated stresses – are undoubtedly critical in determining how stress operates in the offspring: In what aspects of functioning (affective, cognitive, physiological, and behavioral) are there immediate or long-term consequences?

To continue to investigate stress (and support) in the development of children of depressed mothers, but in more child-specific terms, we shift attention to depressed mothers' behavior and to depressed mother–child relationships. We return later to the general family milieu as context for depressed mother–child interactions.

11

DEPRESSED PARENTS: CASE DESCRIPTIONS

Depressed parents do not exhibit a standard set of symptoms. Their personalities, their experiential histories, the current contexts in which they function, and the children in their care are the sources of parental individuality on which depression imposes some commonalities. Depressed parents differ in multiple dimensions, in diverse combinations. Individual depressed mothers and fathers illustrate this diversity.

CASE 1: MRS. K

Mrs. K and 3-year-old Lizzie seemed to be in different worlds as they shared hours in our laboratory apartment.

Lizzie was wiry and athletic with wispy red hair in an uncontrollable mass surrounding her thin face. She approached the novelty of a new experience as if she were wearing rose-colored glasses. She chirped cheerfully, more enthusiastic than most children, as she flitted from one toy to the next. The doll was the prettiest one she had ever seen, and she carried it, at a rapid pace, from high chair, to rocking horse, to rocking chair and back again. She smiled at herself in the mirrors as she ran by, chattering to herself about everything she saw. She was fascinated by a picture on the wall, and squealed excitedly as she noticed many details: "Oh look, the little boy is holding two balloons, but the little girl has an umbrella and a red ribbon in her hair – they match." Her comments were not directed to her mother. She seemed to move in her own space, ignoring her mother.

Mrs. K was a solid, heavy woman with straight blond hair. She was wearing frayed blue jeans and old sneakers. She stomped down the steps and plopped down in the nearest chair. She looked on critically as if she saw the world through dark glasses: "Watch what you're doing." "That's not the way to get off of a rocking horse." "See – you tripped. You're nothing but a klutz." When Lizzie started to open a supply closet door, her mother shouted, "Don't open that door. The boogey man will get you!" Later when Lizzie was building with Legos, her mother yelled, "You're so dumb. That's not the way to do it. It's going to fall over. Make it bigger on the bottom."

At lunchtime, Lizzie's mother heated up some soup and Spaghetti Os and slid them roughly on the table in front of Lizzie. She took some crackers for herself and lounged on the sofa. Mealtimes were not a time of sharing. Lizzie ate enthusiastically, as if she had been presented with a feast: "I love the way these Spaghetti Os slide down. They make my stomach feel like a warm bath. Um Yum."

As usual, Mrs. K had a different view: "Look out. You're spilling. Oh, what a mess you're making." "Ooey, gooey. You're a worm, an ooey, gooey worm," Mrs. K chanted tauntingly. As the morning progressed, there was a rise in pitch and Lizzie's cheerfulness became exaggerated.

In an interview, Lizzie's mother shuddered as she admitted, "I knew it was a big mistake for me to have another child. I didn't want her, but my husband insisted. My first daughter had been an angel. She blended into our lives so easily, but there would never be another one like her."

Mrs. K found her moods fluctuating dramatically and frequently. She found herself going on buying sprees and she told about the large bird cage that she purchased. She would also stay up all night working on projects such as paneling the family room, painting or refinishing furniture. At times like this, she became mean and irritable and would end up arguing and cussing at her husband. No one wanted to be around her.

Since Lizzie's birth, Mrs. K had experienced several depressions. She wouldn't wash or get dressed and could hardly remember doing any cooking or child care. Fortunately, her carpenter husband worked nearby and could check on the children. He also did the housework and grocery shopping, she reported.

Lizzie's moods also varied. Most of the time she was boisterous, chatting and playing actively. Her Dad had a nickname for her: "My super cheerio." When she became angry, however, her anger escalated over several hours to such an intensity that she hyperventilated. Her mother found that the only way she could snap her out of it was to put her in a cold shower.

There was one time when Mrs. K felt so desperate that she thought she might kill herself and the children.

At 6 years, her mother reported, Lizzie played alone most of the time, frequently retreating to her room where she listened to her favorite music, as she counted and recounted her toys. With peers, she was so bossy that they rejected her. She would hit them and then run to her room and cry for 1 to 2 hours.

Her smile had become a grimace. Her giggle was a nervous mannerism. She bit her nails. At 6 years, she was still wearing diapers. She couldn't go to sleep until 10 or 11 p.m. as she watched TV and then had sleepless periods in the middle of the night.

Mealtimes were a torment for her; she was a very picky eater. At lunch, in the apartment, she was the butt of jokes made by her mother and sister as they teased and laughed uproariously. "What food is she going to wear on her shirt today?" they teased, because she was "such a slob." After such teasing, Lizzie put her thumb in the butter and spread the butter on her roll, wiping the rest on her shirt. Then she said, "I don't like to be teased," "Shut up," "Stop it."

Mrs. K complained that Lizzie distorted things so much that it almost seemed as if she was lying.

CASE 2: MR. W

Mr. W was slender and frail. The paleness of his expressionless face was accentuated by an unruly mop of hair. He followed his wife and children into the apartment, giving the barest of responses to overtures of greetings and explanations. When he was spoken to, he looked away, giving almost inaudible, brief answers. When he was in the apartment alone with the children, he tuned them out completely. He looked in the direction of the TV while limply slouched in the chair.

Unsuccessfully, his 5-year-old daughter tried to get his attention. He didn't seem to notice when she sat on his lap playing with a toy. It seemed unusual when he didn't respond in any way when she (also slight in build) climbed on his shoulders and ruffled his hair. Later Mrs. W showed her way of rousing her husband. Although obese, she sat on her little husband's lap and tickled him. The children joined in, sitting on top of mother and father. They all erupted into shrieking, hysterical laughter, a pile of wriggling arms and legs.

In an interview with Mrs. W, we learned that Mr. W often exploded in violent anger. He had thrown a shoe so hard at his 7-year-old that it left a mark on her leg. He had "kicked her on the butt" and pushed her against a wall. When he felt especially angry, he locked the children out of the house. Mrs. W. reported that she had gotten rid of the puppy – fearing for its safety – when he threw it roughly across the room. She also said that her husband is the type who didn't have any friends and chose to work at night to avoid having to interact with people.

At the family's third assessment, Mr. W talked about how angry and "put upon" he felt because he had so much responsibility for child care after school hours while his wife worked. His wife's illness contributed to his burden. He could not meet her needs. He was exhausted and wished that he had never married.

As the children got older, they were better able to meet Mr. W's many demands for neatness and, consequently, he was less violent. He began to be attracted to his daughter's 14-year-old friend, enjoyed her company and conversations. When Mrs. W became jealous and angry, she exploded at her daughter, pushing her and grabbing her by the hair. Her daughter reported this to the Protective Services through school.

The daughter, an "early bloomer" at adolescence, found an older group of teenagers. Both parents were helpless when it came to setting limits on her interest in sexual activity. For Mr. W, it meant one less child around when she went off for Friday and Saturday nights.

CASE 3: MR. Y

Mr. Y galloped up the spiral staircase to the apartment, two steps at a time, followed by 5-year-old John and 9-year-old Marilyn, scurrying as fast as possible to keep up with their father. Mrs. Y trudged slowly, far behind them. After finally arriving at the apartment, she observed her husband's and children's interactions for a few minutes, then turned away and sat down on the sofa in the next room. She opened the newspaper noisily, appearing to be very annoyed by her husband's style of parenting. Tall and thin, Mr. Y towered over his children, giving curt directions and orders, on the correct way to organize the "World Game." John and Marilyn complied immediately.

Both Mr. Y and Mrs. Y were diagnosed with major depression. Both of Mr. Y's parents were also severely depressed. In an interview, Mrs. Y described her husband as very selfish and self-centered; he was never around when she needed companionship or support. He spent a lot of time with his parents. He had recently spent a week in California on a job in filming and looked forward to more work there. In the past, Mr. Y had left for weeks at a time on jobs in other states, including times when his wife was pregnant and about to deliver their babies. She complained that he had not even taken her to the hospital with the last baby. This upset her, because she felt as though he was avoiding her and his responsibility to his family. Additionally annoying to her was his "passive aggressive habit" of beginning renovation projects in their old house but never finishing them. For example, he planned to retile their one bathroom and tore out the old tile, but for months the family walked on boards to get into the bathroom. It was dusty and a real hazard for the children.

When the children were very young, as soon as they began to walk, Mr. Y began his training program for them; his goal was to

125

toughen them up. Seeing them as an extension of himself, he made sure that Marilyn became a tomboy, allowing her to wear only blue jeans.

Over the years, expeditions evolved from hikes and biking to climbing mountains and camping in the rough. They were not to cry if they got hurt or to complain when they got tired. Mr. Y demanded immediate compliance to his explicit rules. The children were expected to go on the trips even when it meant that they missed parties and other activities that they would have preferred. He never informed his wife of his plans.

A dramatic change occurred in Mr. Y during the apartment visit. After "teaching" his children for half an hour, he sat down near his wife. His eyes soon glazed over and there was an unusual flatness to his facial expressions. His wife tried to ask him about the plans for the camping trip the next day. It seemed she was trying to get him to communicate. He didn't seem to hear her and didn't respond.

After the visit, Mrs. Y confirmed that this pattern was typical. He would at times engage in hyperintense activity, using a controlling style with the children to enforce his very high standards, but then suddenly shift and become completely withdrawn and unresponsive. The children had learned to adjust to their father's changes in behavior.

12

THE DEPRESSED MOTHER
AS ENVIRONMENT

How does the depressed mother's behavior, in interaction with other variables, have critical influences on the developmental course and psychiatric and psychosocial outcome of her offspring? Throughout our analyses, the mother has been the independent variable, conceptualized in diagnostic terms of what she is as a depressed person, not a depressed mother. Implicit in the diagnosis of depression, however, is a profile of deficits and dysfunctions that, if exhibited in the role of mother, would be problematic for the child. In this chapter, we examine how the depressed mother expresses her illness in her relationships with her children, and how her behavior influences their behavior and development.

We have imposed two perspectives on the mother. The first is in terms of her "person" characteristics and the second is in terms of her child management and caregiving behavior. In the first framework, the focus is on the mother's personal and interpersonal qualities symptomatic of depression (e.g., depressed mood, irritability, dependency, self-absorption). Her self-absorption and vegetative disturbances in the context of child rearing are the uninvolved or psychologically unavailable mother. The irritability of depression creates an ambience of negativity, and becomes the angry, negative, critical mother. Feelings of worthlessness may be a part of negative communications with her child. The helpless, needy dependency of depression may translate into affective overinvestment in the child or into "parentifying" the child. To the extent that these "person" themes become mothering characteristics, the depressed mother can be viewed as having effects on her child that are direct expressions of her depression.

The second perspective focuses on the mother's socialization and care-giving functions. Does the mother provide the child with

127

a secure and consistent relationship, effective management and regulation of the child's behavior, and experiences supportive of the child's strivings and positive self-regard? Mother's failures in these functions, we assume, are influenced by her symptomatology, but they are not unique to depression.

MEASURES OF THE PARENTING ENVIRONMENT

Our assessments of the parenting environment are based on observed parent–child interaction and interviews.

Observed Behavior Themes in the Mothers

A first objective was to identify mothers on predominant "person" themes. From approximately six hours of videotaped interaction in the apartment, the mother's behavior was rated on her interactions with her child on dimensions of interest and involvement, affective qualities, and facilitative behavior (see chapter 4 for procedure). From these ratings, we derived three Factors:

1. a negative, irritable versus a positive, supportive Factor, with high positive loadings on parent negativity, irritability, and use of strong verbal control, and large negative loadings on parent happy, warm, supportive, and positive toward child. A positive score indicates a negative–irritable style, a negative score indicates a positive–warm style.
2. a facilitative Factor, with high loadings on parent support, involvement, fostering cognitive competence, proactive behavior, and socialization of the child.
3. a considerate control Factor, with high loadings on making control attempts and use of considerate verbal control techniques.

The mothering theme reflecting overinvestment and intense, dependent closeness on the part of the mother was not mea-

128

sured by this rating scheme (although we had initially intended to do so). The coders' orientation was strongly influenced by a framework of normative child-rearing values and variables, where maternal "warmth" is good and interest in child is good. Issues of boundaries between mother and child are not readily perceived in this framework. (For example, one of our most severely depressed mothers who found comfort in prolonged stroking and holding her 2½-year-old was rated high on warmth and attentiveness, not different from effectively functioning mothers.) The pattern of neediness and possessiveness is potentially significant in the transmission of the mother's depression. Clinical inference and integration of behavioral cues are required to pick up the signs of maternal dependency and inseparability from the child. Therefore, an experienced clinician who was unfamiliar with the families coded maternal behavior for evidence of this pattern.

She observed a 30-minute behavior sample (six 5-minute segments) from the same behavior rated by the other coders, and wrote a brief description of the mother–child interaction, relevant to the pattern of engulfing and dependent mothering. Her descriptions were coded by another clinician (independent coding of 17 cases, kappa = .86). These evaluations were made only for the younger sibling group, at the 1½- to 3½-year age period.

We used the Factor scores and the engulfing or enmeshing rating to place the mothers in a hierarchy of "person" categories. The hierarchy and criteria are as follows:

1. *Irritable–negative.* High on the irritable/negative dimension of the irritable versus warm Factor.

2. *Overinvolved or enmeshing.* Clinical coding.

3. *Facilitative.* High on the facilitative Factor and moderate or high in considerate control.

4. *Uninvolved.* Low on both facilitative and control Factor and not high on the warm/positive dimension of the irritable versus warm factor.

5. *Average*, not in any of the preceding categories.

The mother was "forced" into one dominant pattern even though she may be symptomatic in more than one pattern.

In these assessments of mothering, we are essentially giving the mother a primary parental "diagnosis" on the affective message that dominates her relationships with her children. In this "diagnosis," as in a psychiatric diagnosis, we assume that it represents an organizing core in behavior, across time and situations.

Mother as Socializer (Younger Sibling Cohort Only)

In the second framework, we evaluated the mothers on how well they were able to help the young child to regulate/control his or her behavior and affect. Based on observed behavior in the laboratory sessions, the mother's methods of regulating the child and the child's response to each regulation or control attempt were coded (see chapter 4 and Kochanska et al., 1987). Successful maternal management is defined as being above the median in the percentage of control efforts that are followed by the child's compliance (median = 57%).

We also assessed the mother's success in providing a secure base for the child. The attachment paradigm was used to evaluate the mother's relationship with the preschool-age child (see chapter 4).

In summary, the intent of our measures of mothering is to take account of both the person characteristics of the mother (the relationship themes) and her management and caregiving skills. Only conceptually, of course, are they distinct. The distinction is important, however, in trying to understand parental influences on children. The mother's successes in regulating the child and in developing a secure attachment relationship have large components of child influences. The mother's symptomatic themes, we assume, are less child-determined. Our objective is to arrive at an evaluation of the parent as an organized unit.

The full complement of mothering assessments was carried out with the younger sibling group for whom the apartment procedures are especially suited. Mothering themes were evaluated for the older sibling group.

Parenting over Time

Parenting by mother and father was evaluated over the course of childhood. Mothers' themes were coded. Parenting strengths in mother and father were also rated: (a) provides some measure of support or nurturance to the child, and (b) is responsible for the child, although not necessarily with sensitivity. Fathers were coded on violent behavior.

Interviews and log records are the data sources. Coding was done by the liaison staff person with an "interrogator" who imposed a semistandard reporting framework requiring explicit and comprehensive information for assignment to categories. In this way, we utilized the rich, intimate, and detailed accounts and observations that longtime contact with the families produced.

MOTHER'S CHARACTERISTICS

The questions for analyses of parenting are like those for the variables of the larger family environment: What is the nature of the parenting? How are parental qualities influential in the children's development?

Mothering in the Early Years (1½ to 3½ Years)

That the symptoms of depression find expression in mothers' behavior with their children is very apparent (Table 12.1). Approximately half of the depressed mothers exhibit strong symptomatic themes with the child, in contrast to 7% of the well mothers (who are coded as uninvolved). Irritable–negative and dependent–enmeshing themes account for most of the symptomatic patterns in the depressed mothers. Uninvolved mothering describes few of the depressed mothers. Although the laboratory setting may minimize this behavior, it does not preclude it. A small number of mothers are uninvolved to an extreme degree of psychological unavailability to the child – in zombie-like behavior.

In regulation of child behavior, bipolar and well mothers are

131

Table 12.1 *Mothers' behavior patterns (% of mothers)*

Mother's behavior patterns	Mother's diagnosis		
	Well	Bipolar	Unipolar
With younger siblings at 1½ to 3½ years			
Symptomatic	7	42	50
Irritable–negative	0	15	17
Uninvolved	7	8	10
Enmeshed	0	19	24
Asymptomatic	93	58	50
Facilitative	43	35	31
"Average"	50	23	19
Regulation of child			
Successful	60	64	38
Unsuccessful	40	36	62
Attachment relationship			
Secure	67	40	62
Insecure	33	60	38
With older siblings at 5 to 8 years			
Symptomatic	23	36	21
Irritable–negative	10	18	19
Uninvolved	13	18	2
Asymptomatic	77	64	78
Facilitative	47	32	47
"Average"	30	32	31

equally successful (64% and 60%, respectively). The unipolar mothers least often (38%) achieve success. In detailed analyses of the interactions of these mothers with their children, Kochanska et al. (1987) describe some of the qualities that contribute to mothers' failures in regulating their children. Mothers who are unsuccessful tend to avoid confrontation with the child, set up situations of control that cannot be resolved, and tend not to extend effort and perseverance into their regulation of the child.

On attachment patterns, the mothers of the three diagnostic groups again line up differently. Insecure attachment appears in

60% of the bipolar group, and in approximately a third of the unipolar depressed and well mother groups.

Mothering of the Older Siblings (5 to 8 Years)

Symptomatic mothering themes in interactions in the apartment with the older siblings do not differ in frequency in depressed and well mothers (27% and 25%, respectively); however, from a few of the depressed mothers there are devastating encounters with these children in which denigration and hostility are open and intense (see Margaret in chapter 5).

Summary

We see that the mother's "person" qualities of depression translate into qualities of her relationships with her child. The specific translations vary among depressed mothers. In child-rearing "practices," too, there are difficulties.

Theoretically, capacities for healthy transition into childhood are being compromised on multiple fronts: (1) depressed mother's negativity is undercutting the child's positive feelings about self and others; (2) enmeshment is complicating autonomy strivings; (3) uninvolvement and feelings of helplessness are providing little help to the child in regulating his/her behaviors; and (4) the attachment relationship is being embedded in the strong affective and interactional qualities of depression. This early timing of influences has the potential for establishing impairing patterns of child behavior, and setting the direction of the developmental path.

Depressed Parenting Throughout Childhood

The qualities of depressed mothering continue into childhood and adolescence. There are strong elements of negativity and anger in the mothers' approach to life and to the children (see Table 12.2). Nearly half of both unipolar and bipolar depressed mothers are rated angry/irritable. Approximately 40% of the fathers add sub-

Table 12.2 *Parenting behavior in families of depressed mothers*
(% of families)

Parenting behavior[a]	Mother's diagnosis	
	Bipolar	Unipolar
Mother is angry–irritable	42.3	42.9
Mother's borderline personality		
boundary issues	69.2	33.3 ($p<.01$)
unstable enthusiasms	61.5	26.2 ($p<.01$)
impulsive behavior	65.5	47.6
Father is violent	38.5	42.9
Mother is unavailable		
to younger sibling	19.2	14.3
to older sibling	18.2	9.5
Mother is responsible but not sensitive		
to younger sibling	30.8	45.2
to older sibling	40.9	33.3
Mother provides some nurturing		
to younger sibling	30.8	38.1
to older sibling	31.8	40.5
Father assumes little consistent responsibility	46.2	61.9
Father provides some nurturing		
to younger sibling	69.2	45.2
to older sibling	63.6	42.8
Father rejects		
younger sibling	19.2	26.2
older sibling	31.8	14.3

[a]Parent may be classified in several categories

stantially to the "angry" environments, with recurrent violent behavior. Psychological unavailability of the mother is reflected not only in the ratings of unavailability but also in the ratings of "responsible but not sensitive" to child's needs. Roughly a third of the mothers are given this rating. Many fathers, especially in families with unipolar depressed mothers, are not consistently responsible parents (62% in families of unipolar mothers and 46% in families of bipolar mothers).

The high tallies of risk in the parenting patterns must not obscure the fact that there are dedicated depressed parents who are struggling to provide for their children. These parents are confronted with the tasks of dealing with their highly troubled children as well as with their own problems. Mothers in a third of the families are seen as providing some positive nurturing to their children, and fathers are, to some extent, stabilizing, nurturing figures for their children in two-thirds of the families of bipolar mothers and slightly less than half of the families of unipolar mothers.

Overall, parenting dysfunctions in middle and later childhood are, in many ways, similar in families of unipolar and bipolar mothers. The borderline personality characteristics observed often among bipolar mothers (consistent with the personality inventory assessments reported earlier) are one significant difference.

Continuity in Mothering Themes

The persisting risks in maternal behavior are apparent also in following the behavioral course of the individual mother (see Table 12.3). Of the initially negative mothers, 92% continue to be rated angry, and none becomes supportive. Of initially enmeshing mothers, 60% join the theme of negative–irritable parenting, and 40% continue to be noted as "using" the child in highly dependent and self-gratifying ways in later childhood. Although the majority of initially facilitative mothers continue to be supportive or responsible, more than a quarter of them are also angry mothers. Mothers who were uninvolved with their toddlers do not become highly involved as their children get older.

With the older siblings, the course of mothers' parenting is similar. Angry–irritable mothers continue to be so throughout childhood, and mothers who were rated facilitative or average when they were first observed, in a third of the cases, are angry mothers in later childhood.

The drift toward increasing numbers of depressed mothers characterized by negativity and irritability suggests that this expression of depression may be accentuated over the childhood years. In this sense, the parenting becomes harsher.

135

Table 12.3 *Continuity/discontinuity in qualities of parenting by depressed mothers (% of mothers)*

	Mothering through childhood				
Early pattern of mothering	Some positive support	Responsible not sensitive	Angry-irritable[a]	Uninvolved or unavailable[a]	"Uses" child[a]
With younger siblings at 1½ to 3½ years					
Facilitative	63.6	27.3	27.3	4.6	14.6
"Average"	35.7	57.1	28.6	7.1	28.6
Irritable–negative	0.0	36.4	90.9	45.5	0.0
Uninvolved	16.7	66.7	0.0	0.0	0.0
Enmeshed	26.7	33.3	60.0	26.7	40.0
With older siblings at 5 to 8 years					
Facilitative	51.9	37.0	37.0	7.4	11.1
"Average"	30.0	45.0	30.0	10.0	10.0
Irritable–negative	8.3	25.0	83.3	33.3	8.3
Uninvolved	60.0	20.0	0.0	0.0	0.0

[a]Mother may be rated "angry," "unavailable," and "uses child."

PREDICTIONS FROM MOTHERING CHARACTERISTICS

Do the mothering differences make a difference in children's development? Our first step in analyses of the consequences of depressed mothering is to follow each of the elements in our conceptualization of depressed mother – her interactional patterns (symptomatic or asymptomatic), her regulation of the child, and the attachment pattern – for their separate associations with later problems in the child.

Predictions from the First Three Years

"Early experience," especially the first three years, carries the overtones of significance for the child's future. If maternal depression interferes with mothering in this period, does this impairment influence the child's development, and, if so, by what mechanisms?

Depressed Mothers' Interactional Themes and Children's Later Problems. This aspect of early experience is predictive of the developmental course. Specific types of symptomatic mothering in the first three years are predictive of children's disruptive disorders (Exact $p < .05$). Children experiencing negative–irritable mothering have the highest rate of disruptive disorders appearing at some time in the course of development (82%), followed by children of enmeshing mothers (73%), of "average" mothers (57%), of facilitative mothers (36%), and of uninvolved mothers (17%). There is no similar pattern of association for diagnoses of anxiety and depression.

Mothers' Regulation of Child Behavior and Children's Later Problems. Mother's early failure in regulating child behavior is also predictive of children's later problems. For children of well mothers, the pattern is dramatic, with 83% of children of unsuccessful and only 11% of children of successful mothers having a problem (Exact $p < .0001$). For children of depressed mothers, 81%

of the children whose mothers were unsuccessful and 70% whose mothers were successful in regulating the child are diagnosed with problems ("any" problem) at the T3,4 assessments (χ^2 (1) = 4.86, $p < .05$). Children of unsuccessful unipolar mothers are more likely to have recurrent depression than children of successful mothers (29% vs. 0%) and less likely never to be depressed than children of successful mothers (25% vs. 60%) (Exact $p < .05$).

The Attachment Relationship and Children's Later Problems. Contrary to theoretical expectation, securely attached children of depressed mothers are more likely to have a diagnosis of depression at the T3,4 assessment than are insecurely attached children (44% vs. 23%, χ^2 (1) = 3.82, $p < .05$). Attachment is also related to recurrent depression; 21% of securely attached and 7% of insecurely attached children of depressed mothers have had recurrent depression (χ^2 (1) = 5.21, $p <.05$). Problem frequencies in securely and insecurely attached children of well mothers do not differ significantly.

Predictions for the Older Siblings

The data do not permit a full exploration of predictions from early mothering for the older siblings (they were already between 5 and 8 years when they came into the study). However, the older children with negative depressed mothers (like their younger siblings) are more likely (92%) than other children (20% to 70%) to have disruptive problems sometime in childhood (Exact $p < .05$).

Comments on Depressed Mothers' Characteristics in Relation to Offspring Development

In chapter 8, we found that each of the diagnostic qualities of mother's depression (e.g., age of onset, chronicity) is significantly associated with offspring problems. We are seeing a replay here of many significant associations between single properties of the depressed mothers' behavior in the early years and children's later problems. The difficulty common to both sets of findings is that one cannot address the question with which this chapter began – *how* do *interacting* factors have critical influences? In the next analyses, we examine *patterns* of maternal characteristics as predictors of offspring outcomes.

PREDICTIONS FROM PATTERNS OF MOTHERING

The child experiences the mother as an organized entity. We have tried to capture this entity in the patterns of mothering. We are interested in how these patterns of variables act together in influencing child behavior. For example, one might find that unsuccessful regulation of the child by a symptomatic mother is differently predictive of child problems from unsuccessful regulation by an asymptomatic mother.

Mothering Themes and Regulation of the Child

We did not find a significant interaction of mothering themes and regulation for children's problems at the end point of our assessments. Unsuccessful regulation of the child is equally predictive of child problems for symptomatic mothers and asymptomatic mothers.

Mothering Themes and Attachment

There is a significant interaction of mothering themes and attachment pattern, however, for child outcomes of anxiety ($\chi^2(1) = 4.05$, $p < .05$), disruptive problems ($\chi^2(1) = 21.20, p < .0001$), and "any" problem ($\chi^2(1) = 10.95, p < .001$), but not depression. A smaller proportion of children securely attached to asymptomatic mothers than of children insecurely attached have diagnoses of anxiety and disruptive disorders (in line with attachment theory) (see Table 12.4). Children securely attached to symptomatic mothers more often develop later problems than do children insecurely attached to symptomatic mothers (contrary to theory).

Table 12.4 *Children's problems in relation to depressed mother's behavior and attachment pattern*
(% of children)

			Problems at T3,4 assessments			
Mother–child relationship	n	Depressed	Anxious	Disruptive	"Any" problem
Symptomatic mothers					
Secure attachment	14	50.0	71.4	78.6	100.0
Insecure attachment	18	22.2	33.3	44.4	66.7
Asymptomatic mothers					
Secure attachment	22	40.9	36.4	22.7	72.7
Insecure attachment	13	23.1	46.2	61.5	76.9
Irritable–negative mothers					
Secure attachment	3	66.7	66.7	100.0	100.0
Insecure attachment	8	25.0	37.5	62.5	75.0
Enmeshed mothers					
Secure attachment	10	50.0	70.0	80.0	100.0
Insecure attachment	5	0.0	40.0	40.0	60.0

Uninvolved mothers					
Secure attachment	1	0.0	100.0	0.0	100.0
Insecure attachment	5	40.0	20.0	20.0	60.0
Facilitative mothers					
Secure attachment	13	38.5	38.5	15.4	76.9
Insecure attachment	8	12.5	50.0	50.0	75.0
"Average" mothers					
Secure attachment	9	44.0	33.3	33.3	66.7
Insecure attachment	5	40.0	40.0	80.0	80.0

This interaction of mother's symptomatic or asymptomatic behavior and the attachment relationship in affecting children's development is detailed in Table 12.4. Anxiety, disruptive disorders, and "any problem" appear more often in the securely attached than in the insecurely attached children of each type of symptomatic mother. Disruptive problems with uninvolved mothers are an exception. With facilitative and "average" mothers, anxiety and disruptive disorders appear less often in the securely attached children. When recurrence of problems over the course of childhood is the criterion, the findings are virtually identical.

As previously noted, for children's depression, the main effect of attachment is significant, regardless of the depressed mother's symptomatic theme.

Further interactive influences among the three facets of parenting may be important in the development of children's problems. The number of cases is too small for reliable assessment. Hence, the data in Table 12.5 are presented only as descriptive and suggestive of hypotheses.

At a descriptive level, when mothers are symptomatic and attachment is secure, high rates of depression and disruptive disorders occur, regardless of mother's effectiveness in regulating the child (rows 5 and 7). Higher rates of depression occur also with the depressed asymptomatic mother when attachment is secure (rows 1 and 3) than when attachment is insecure. Rates of anxiety and disruptive disorders are high with symptomatic mothers with secure attachment and unsuccessful regulation (row 7); and with asymptomatic mothers with insecure attachment and unsuccessful regulation (row 4).

The Significance of Patterns of Variables

We need now to bring together what we have learned by having considered the several aspects of the mother's behavior as the pattern in which the child experiences her. We see from the data that specific combinations of maternal behavior affect children differently, as the various facets of maternal behavior affect the functional significance of other facets. This process goes undetected when each variable is observed by itself in relation to the child's behavior. The fact that any single variable can have very different "meanings," depending on its context, puts constraints on interpretation of single-variable analyses. Systematic investigation of diverse patterns of variables and their outcomes begins to build bases for inferences regarding mechanisms. The interaction of the mother's symptomatic qualities and attachment in influencing offspring outcome is only one example.

PREDICTIONS FROM PARENTING BEHAVIOR AND FAMILY ENVIRONMENTS

Because mother–child relationships have had the focus, the family has been ignored. We now view the two sets of data in combination. Do the mothering characteristics in combination with family stress increase the predictability of children's outcomes?

We used regression analyses as one approach to this question. For this analysis, we used the broadest assessment of child disorders, the child's symptoms on the DICA classified as total symptoms, internalizing and externalizing symptoms. Presence or absence of high interpersonal family stress was forced into the model. Mothering variables were entered in the stepwise fashion, using alpha = .05 as the criterion. Symptomatic mothering, attachment, and regulation of the child were all entered, as well as an interaction term for each characteristic with stress.

No mothering characteristic alone increased the predictability (R^2) of the regression, but each of the interaction terms significantly increased R^2 for one or more of the measures of the child (see Table 12.6). High family stress in combination with secure attachment and symptomatic mothering best predicts total symptoms as well as total internalizing symptoms. Externalizing counts are less well predicted. High family stress alone is not a significant predictor, but stress in the presence of a mother's lack of success in early regulation of the child provides some predictability.

It is for children of symptomatic negative–irritable or enmeshed

Table 12.5 *Children's problems in relation to depressed mother's symptomatic pattern, regulation of child, and attachment pattern (% of children)*

| Mother–child relationship | n | Problems at T3,4 | | |
		Depressed	Anxious	Disruptive
Asymptomatic mothers				
Successful regulation				
Secure attachment	11	27.3	36.4	18.2
Insecure attachment	7	14.3	28.6	28.6
Unsuccessful regulation				
Secure attachment	8	50.0	25.0	25.0
Insecure attachment	6	33.3	66.7	100.0
Symptomatic mothers				
Successful regulation				
Secure attachment	6	50.0	16.7	66.7
Insecure attachment	7	28.6	28.6	28.6
Unsuccessful regulation				
Secure attachment	8	50.0	62.5	87.5
Insecure attachment	11	18.2	36.4	54.5

mothers that family stress creates havoc. The mean internalizing scores for the negative–irritable/high stress and enmeshed/high stress combinations are 21.4 and 20.4, whereas, in the other maternal groups, the scores with high stress range from 13.6 to 14.3. Mean scores in the conditions of low family stress range from 7.7 (with negative–irritable mothers) to 13.0 (uninvolved mothers).

SUMMARY

The behavior of depressed mothers clearly influences the development of psychopathology in the offspring. Moreover, the specific problem areas are predictable. Data on the patterns of early experiences with the depressed mother suggest specific mecha-

Table 12.6 Stepwise regression analysis assessing contributions of mothering and family stress to children's symptom counts (younger siblings)

DICA symptom counts	Significant variables and interaction terms	F	p	Contribution to R^2	Standardized beta
Total symptoms	High stress	7.01	<.01	.09	2.64
	Attachment X stress	6.68	<.05	.09	-2.58[a]
	Symptomatic X stress	4.28	<.05	.06	2.06
Internalizing symptoms	High stress	7.94	<.01	.14	2.82
	Attachment X stress	6.93	<.05	.08	-2.63
	Symptomatic X stress	5.95	<.05	.07	2.44
Externalizing symptoms	High stress	5.22	<.05	.03	2.28[b]
	Regulation X stress	3.95	<.05	.06	-1.99

[a]The negative coefficient indicates lower symptom counts for the insecurely attached than the securely attached, in the presence of high stress.
[b]High stress makes a significant contribution only in the presence of the regulation by stress term.

145

nisms through which the child's vulnerability to maladaptive behavior is increased.

Our conceptualization of mothering includes both the direct effects of mother's diagnosis (her symptomatology) and the indirect effects of her illness on essential rearing functions. Early experiences of the child, by both avenues, are significantly linked to later specific problems in the child. However, the high continuity in symptomatic aspects of mothering throughout childhood modifies interpretations of processes connecting early experience to later outcomes. Not all of the influence is from the early years.

Uninvolved mothering, a quality often emphasized in describing depressed mothers, is not predictive from our observational data. However, from the interview data on personality disorders, we see that maternal avoidant personality is associated with repeated disruption problems in the children.

"Uninvolved" is not a "pure" quality of the mother, and does not have a clear meaning without knowledge of its context. "Uninvolved" does not specify mother's concurrent behavior. The mother may be in a severe episode of depression and be uninvolved; or she may be totally absorbed in herself in manic grandiosity; or she may be overwhelmed by her anger with her husband. Effects on her children are likely to be influenced by her behavior in her unavailability.

It may be, too, that children are better able to cope with mother's unavailability than with other symptomatic mothering qualities that direct behavior to them. As was often observed, the children of depressed mothers find a substitute caregiver or another committed relationship, or develop early responsibility for themselves.

Our conceptualization of mothering was intended as an assessment of the "necessary" environment for a child to develop adaptively, and as a probe into how far this necessary environment breaks down with maternal depression. This view of environment suggests additive influences, but the data indicate clearly that this is not the best representation of influences, that the interaction of influences is important. "Protective" conditions in the company of certain other conditions can become "risks" (and vice versa).

146

The findings have implications for investigating parenting influences in normal as well as psychopathological development. Single dimensions of parent behavior, without considering other relationships and contexts, can result in misleading conclusions and underestimate parental influences. Developmental research on child rearing and family influences on children's development has rarely taken on the difficult task of dealing with the multiplicity of parental variables that together act on the child. Such multiplicity is strikingly evident in families with parental psychopathology. They are no less likely to exist and significantly affect rearing processes in normal families.

13

THE CHILD AS A VARIABLE IN DEVELOPMENT AND OUTCOME

Children do not choose or make their family environments, at least not those characterized by mother's manic episodes, deep depression, continuing gloom, parental fighting, father's violence and alcoholism. Children do not choose the attributes and predispositions with which they are endowed. However, children are active agents on their own behalf. They bring to the environment of maternal depression their individuality in perceiving, acting, and reacting. In these ways, children contribute to their own course. Emma, Jeremy, and Adam illustrate this process.

Emma, at 15 years, recounts her mother's all-night "activity jags," her sleeping through the next day. One time, she recalls, her mother dressed up in overly tight clothes and heavy makeup, and walked out on the street hailing cars. Emma was so scared: "I ran into the house and cleaned everything." She verbalized that she was going to be "the good person"; she knew her family was "crazy" and she was ashamed.

Jeremy, age 2½, arrived on the run and jumped down the last two steps into the apartment – squeals of excitement announced "I'm here and ready to go." His mother stood in the doorway watching him dash from room to room and back again. It wasn't long before Jeremy discovered the "Temptation Table" with mother's instructions not to touch. He refused to obey his mother, although she tried many times to control him. Through the morning, Jeremy and his mother were at odds with each other. Jeremy rejected her invitations to play or hear a story. Mealtime was a disaster. The airplane spoon arriving with food was gunned down. Food was spilled accidentally and much of it ended on the floor. Jeremy won! Jeremy pestered his mother when she withdrew her attention by reading a book, resting, or talking on the phone. During the morning the tension mounted. Jeremy anxiously chewed toys instead of playing with them. As he approached the "Temptation Table," Jeremy held his bottom and then ran to sit on the sofa to protect himself from the spanking his mother threatened.

For *Adam* each year was worse than the last one. His mother yelled at him and he yelled back over every little thing. When he was 14 years old, she began to renovate his room (without asking him), stripping wallpaper and painting a mural in garish colors. She thought she was an artist. She went on buying sprees – new curtains, bedspreads, and furniture in styles he didn't like. She even got rid of his favorite lumpy chair. She wouldn't listen to him. He wanted to lift weights. That was all he wanted. How could that be too expensive? One night his frustration and anger boiled over. He trashed his room, kicked the door until it fell off its hinges, and punched a hole in the middle of the mural. He turned on all the lights in the house and left. He didn't return that night. The police found him the next morning and brought him home.

The mothers of Emma, Jeremy, and Adam are acting on and with very different children, and the children are experiencing their mothers in their own ways, and providing different returns. Their individuality has a place in the processes linking parental and offspring psychopathology.

Our objective in this chapter is to bring into the analyses characteristics of the child that interact with maternal diagnosis, family environment, and depressed mother's behavior. Parent-to-child direction of influences, a framework that has dominated research, whether of normal or psychopathological development, is not easily revised to incorporate child-to-parent influences. Moreover, turning to child effects runs the risk of simply reversing the one-way direction of effects. Neither of the one-way frameworks fully addresses the processes implied in a conceptualization of child and parent engaged in reciprocal interactions and influences. Our analyses of the child as a variable in development are one-way and two-way formulations of influences, as the data allow. We have investigated gender and temperament as major child variables.

GENDER AS A VARIABLE IN CHILDREN'S PROBLEMS

We begin with the most evident child difference. In theories, beliefs, and empirical data, the gender of offspring of depressed parents is a relevant variable. The repeated finding of higher rates of unipolar depression in women than in men accents gender as a significant variable. Not at all clear, however, are the paths to these differences. Explanations range from biological to social sex role origins. From her review of the literature, Nolen-Hoeksema (1987) concludes that none of the explanations adequately accounts for the gender difference in depression in adults.

With regard to depressive disorders of males and females in the childhood years, the data are not conclusive. Nolen-Hoeksema notes that gender differences emerge after puberty. Likewise, Weissman, Gammon, John, Merikangas, Warner, Prusoff, and Sholomskas (1987) report a greater ratio of girls to boys after 12 years.

A number of studies have examined the symptoms of depression exhibited by boys and girls. According to Kovacs (1980), depressive symptoms prior to puberty tend toward acting out behavior in boys, and toward negative self-evaluations in girls. Both boys and girls manifest sadness. There is little research information concerning the experiences of boys and girls growing up with a depressed mother that might influence the kinds of problems that they develop.

Our analyses take us first to the problems exhibited by boys and girls; then to their growing-up experiences.

Problems of Boys and Girls

We find no simple, generalizable gender differences in the children's problems across development. Age, type of problem, and mother's diagnosis enter into the differences.

There are gender differences in disruptive disorders, but they do not "favor" the same gender at each age. Boys are more disruptive than girls at 5 to 8 years old (22% vs. 10%) and at 8 to 11 years (35% vs. 18%), regardless of mother's diagnosis. At ages 15 to 19, boys of well mothers continue to have more disruptive problems than girls of well mothers (23% vs. 0%); however, girls of depressed mothers have more disruptive, acting-out problems than boys of depressed mothers, (29% of girls of unipolar mothers, 54% of girls of bipolar mothers, and 17% of boys of both unipolar and bipolar mothers). Findings on recurrent disruptive problems are similar. Recurrent problems over the course of development are more frequent in boys than girls of well mothers (21% vs. 0%), but more frequent in girls than boys of depressed mothers (38% vs. 24%; all $p < .05$) The developmental course of disruptive problems firmly puts the older girls of depressed mothers at high risk.

We find no gender differences in depression. But with anxiety there is again a gender by mother diagnosis interaction ($p < .06$). Of the girls of unipolar depressed mothers, 38% have anxiety problems at 5 to 8 years compared with 14% of the younger girls of well mothers and none of the girls of bipolar depressed mothers. The boys' anxiety at this age is not related to mother's diagnosis (range 19% to 25%). Anxiety in gender comparisons, as in other comparisons, is least consistent or predictable in rate and course.

It is in the comorbidity of disruptive problems and depression or anxiety that the girls of depressed mothers, at ages 11 to 19, stand out in high frequency: 62% of the girls and 40% of the boys of depressed mothers, and 21% of the boys and 0% of the girls of well mothers (gender by maternal diagnosis interaction ($\chi^2(2) = 6.67, p < .01$). We look now for possible developmental precursors of this high vulnerability in the girls.

Gender and Parenting by Depressed Mothers

Growing up with a depressed mother may carry different risks for boys and girls because of different experiences, particularly differences in the relationship with the mother. Indeed, a gender difference is suggested in a detailed analysis of maternal control behavior by Kochanska et al. (1987). They describe depressed mothers' particular difficulty in regulating their preschool-age daughters.

This observation is interesting in light of our earlier finding (chapter 12) that the mother's failure to help the child to reach the developmental milestone of socialized self-control was significantly related to later disruptive problems. Although this effect holds for both genders, it is for the girls that it is more pronounced. When the mother was unsuccessful in early regulation of the child, 71% of the girls are disruptive at ages 8 to 15 years, compared with 26% when she was successful ($\chi^2(2) = 6.62$, $p <$ .01). For boys the parallel figures are 58% and 42%.

In comparisons of parenting patterns with boys and girls in early childhood and over the childhood years, we found no other gender differences in the qualities of mother–child relationships, and no significant interactions of gender with attachment or early symptomatic mothering in relation to child problems. One exception is that fathers in families with depressed mothers are more frequently rejecting of sons than of daughters (younger cohort) (Exact $p < .01$).

Not finding a general gender difference in family experiences does not rule out gender as an influential factor in some and perhaps many families. Gender is a strong determinant of who is favored, victimized, or "used." But it may be a boy or a girl, depending on family value systems and stereotypes, specific needs of the parent, and special characteristics of the children. In one family, only "maleness" is valued, and even the girls must behave like boys. There are families in which all the responsibilities of household management and care of younger siblings fall to the older daughter. In other circumstances, the daughter is singled out protectively by the father. For some mothers, the son becomes an emotional substitute for a hostile or absent spouse, or the avenue for family achievement when the father has failed. These gender-determined risks or protections are not visible in group comparisons.

Depressed mothers sometimes explicitly draw their offspring

into their depression by identifying characteristics in the child that are like their own (e.g., "She looks like me; she acts just like me when I was 13"; "She, her grandmother and I are all alike"; "I told him he had a 75% chance of becoming bipolar"). This information is not easily systematically obtainable, but in families in which explicit statements were volunteered by the mother, boys and girls appear to be equally involved.

Among depressed mothers with strong dependency needs, demands on the child for nurturance involve both boys and girls. Fathers in some of the families develop similar dependent relationships with their daughters in the adolescent years. The daughter reminds the father of his happy, sparkling wife in the first years of their marriage. The daughters become close companions of their fathers, with housekeeping and management responsibilities "beyond their years." In terms of the idiosyncrasies of the individual depressed parent or family, the gender of the child can be the variable that significantly shapes the child's family experiences.

We conclude from the findings on the problems and family treatment of male and female offspring of depressed mothers that there is not a uniform main gender influence. At the same time, gender frequently plays a significant role, via different avenues. With girls of depressed mothers, there is a reappearing theme of regulatory difficulties – appearing early and late in development. How much this behavior is an expression of inherent child qualities and how much it is a result of depressed mothers' difficulties in relationships with daughters is a question our data cannot answer. Idiosyncratic family values and parent needs make gender an important variable.

TEMPERAMENT AS A VARIABLE IN CHILDREN'S PROBLEMS

Next to gender, children's temperament is most readily apparent, even to the "uninformed." A child's "behavioral style" is generally obvious at a very early age, and it tends to remain relatively stable. Although the criteria, content, and assessment of temperament are not fully agreed upon (Kagan, 1984; Rutter, 1989c) reactional dispositions have long been recognized as qualities that differentiate children. The tender-minded and tough-minded child, the "difficult" and the "laid-back" are some of the distinguishing temperament types. It is hypothesized that these qualities are variously predisposing or protective with regard to the development of children's problems. It has been suggested, for example, that children of behaviorally inhibited temperament are predisposed to anxiety disorders (Biederman, Rosenbaum, Hirshfeld, Faraone, Boldue, Gersten, Merringer, Kagen, Snidman, & Resnick 1990).

Measures of Temperament

To assess children's temperament, we used the child's behavior in the apartment (T1), CBCL items, clinical notes of the psychiatrist, and the mother's retrospective descriptions of her child in infancy and prior to entry into the study.

To measure shyness, we used the Kagan et al. (1984) paradigm for assessing behavioral inhibition (see chapter 4) (for the younger sibling only), the mother's report of child's early characteristics, and the shyness items on the CBCL. To measure the "difficult" child, we used observations of the child's irritability, needing control, and oppositional behavior. Pleasant, sociable temperament is based on frequent ratings of happy and affectionate expression, few ratings of sad, anxious, and irritable, and low need for control (see chapter 4 for procedures).

For each temperament, we created a summary score. Then we grouped the children as high, medium, or low on each characteristic, based on the distributions of the summary score. Finally, we classified the children in one of five temperament groups, based on extreme scores, as "difficult," "shy," "pleasant sociable," "low pleasant sociable," or "average." For some analyses, we grouped children as having a "problem" temperament (difficult, shy, or low pleasant sociable) or an "easy" temperament (sociable or average).

154

Predictions from Child Temperament

We are interested in child temperament in two respects: First, does it have a direct effect on the nature and number of child problems? Second, temperament, in a limited way, defines the affective–social qualities that the child brings to the mother. How do mother–child dyads composed of different qualities of child temperament and different qualities of mother influence the child's development? Are there reciprocal influences between mother and child that influence child development?

Just as child temperament is assumed to have some inherent or constitutional basis, as well as some overlay of, or susceptibility to, environmental influences, so, too, mother's disposition, as expressed in her symptomatology, is assumed to have an inherent quality, and also an experiential overlay. The question then is: As these two "person" qualities are paired in a mother–child relationship, what are the processes by which they influence each other and through which they enter into the child's development?

Preliminary to these analyses, we compared children by mothers' diagnoses and found no significant differences in temperament (53%, 62%, and 57% of children of well, bipolar, and unipolar mothers with problem temperament). There are no significant gender differences in problem temperament (59% of boys, 55% of girls) when controlling for mother's diagnosis.

Problematic child temperament, when considered alone, is a predictor in families of depressed mothers only of disruptive disorders, and only in the younger siblings (T3,4 assessment). Low pleasant sociable children ($n = 23$), shy children ($n = 10$), and difficult children ($n = 7$) have disruptive problems in 61%, 70%, and 57% of the cases, respectively. Only 22% of the sociable children ($n = 9$) and 26% of the average children ($n = 19$) have disruptive problems ($\chi^2 = 9.67$, $p < .05$). In the well families, more children of problem temperament than of easy temperament have a disorder at T3,4 (44% and 36%, respectively), but the difference is not significant.

155

Table 13.1 *Mother–child dyads and children's problems*
(% of children of depressed mothers)

Mother–child dyad	*n*	Problem present at T3,4	Comorbid problems at T3,4	Recurrent problems
Younger siblings, 8 to 15 years				
Symptomatic mother				
problem temperament child	24	92	67	75
easy temperament child	8	50	13	38
Asymptomatic mother				
problem temperament child	16	75	31	38
easy temperament child	20	70	30	35
Older siblings, 11 to 19 years				
Symptomatic mother				
problem temperament child	11	100	73	91
easy temperament child	6	100	33	50
Asymptomatic mother				
problem temperament child	23	70	30	65
easy temperament child	24	92	38	88

Predictions from the Depressed Mother–Child Dyad to Later Child Problems

Although child temperament does not have a compelling role in development, when considered by itself, it does have a significant role when considered in interaction with mothering variables. In the dyad, we observe the reciprocal influences of child's and mother's dispositions on each other (see Table 13.1). Dyads of symptomatic mothers with children of problem temperament predict high rates of problems at T3,4. In these dyads, 67% of the younger children have comorbid internalizing and externalizing problems, and only 8% are without a diagnosis. Neither mother nor child brings a protective quality to this relationship. In these dyads, children with negative or enmeshing mothers fare worst, with 90% and 100%, respectively, having problems (8 to 15 years). In dyads of symptomatic mother and easy temperament, 50% of the children have a diagnosis. Child temperament can be credited as the moderating influence.

Dyads of asymptomatic mothers paired with children of problematic or easy temperaments have very similar outcomes; 25% and 30%, respectively, are without diagnoses at T3,4. The asymptomatic mothers appear to moderate the effects of child problem temperaments.

Findings are similar in predicting children's recurrent problems. The interaction between type of mother and child temperament is significant ($\chi^2(2) = 8.40$, $p < .05$). Children of asymptomatic mothers, with and without problem temperaments, again do not differ significantly in their problem patterns. In the presence of symptomatic mothering, 75% of the children with problem temperaments and 38% of the children with easy temperaments have recurrent problems.

Findings on the younger children are only partly replicated with the older siblings. All of the older children with symptomatic mothers have some problem at T3,4, regardless of the child's temperament. Children of problem temperaments, with symptomatic mothers, have a higher rate of comorbid problems (73%) than children of all other dyads (approximately 33%) (temperament by mother symptomatic, at a trend level, $\chi^2(4) = 2.92$, $p < .10$).

As we compared dyads in the younger cohort, we found that the mother's symptomatic status and the child's temperament are not independent. Some 60% of the young children with problem temperaments and 29% of the children with easy temperaments have symptomatic mothers (Exact $p = .01$). Our a posteriori hypothesis is that the attributes of both mother and child, when brought together in a relationship, result in an escalation of these qualities in both mother and child. This kind of process could well have taken place in the years prior to our observations.

CHILDREN'S BEHAVIOR AS A
SOURCE OF STRESS

Our data allow several other observations of child effects. We observed in the case descriptions in chapters 5 and 9 how the children burden their stressed parents with their own serious problems. Parents' energies, skills, and concerns are claimed by the crises and risks created by the children's disturbed behavior.

Also, in the data referred to earlier concerning depressed mothers' difficulties in controlling their daughters, mothers were experiencing stress. They responded to this stress variously – with withdrawal in the face of their daughter's opposition, dysregulation of their own affect, escalated tension. Clearly, the mother's behavior was being affected, at the moment, by the child's behavior, in ways that could interfere with continuing interactions with the child. We wondered: Might there be longer-term consequences that stress-generating children have on their environment? A small bit of evidence suggests that there are. We found that child stressors of noncompliance with the depressed mother's control attempts are not only correlated with ratings of family stress in the same period of time (tau-b $= .25$, $p < .05$); they are also correlated with family stress three years later (tau-b $= .29$, $p < .02$) and six years later. (A similar association appears in the well families; tau-b $= .45$, $p < .05$.) The processes we have inferred are child stressor characteristics interacting with mother's vulnerabilities, thereby contributing to continuing stressful relationships in the family and, in turn, negatively affecting offspring problems.

The co-occurrence of stress in family functioning, difficult mother–child relationships, and child's disturbed behavior plainly demonstrates the many interacting influences and the multiple sources and directions of influences.

CHILDREN'S METHODS OF COPING

From a quite different perspective, we consider the individuality and the active roles of children in their ways of coping with sur-

158

vival under the conditions of risk and stress associated with maternal depression.

When we first saw 3½-year-old Megan and her 7-year-old sister, children of a rapid-cycling bipolar mother, they had already learned to turn to each other for care and security. They never asked their mother for help or attention in the apartment; they made their own way through the morning. An 8-year-old boy of a bipolar mother described his attic hideaway, to which he retreats when the fighting and yelling get too bad. A teenager weathers her despair by writing poetry, while her younger brother goes to his grandparents' house whenever he can. All the "craziness" in her family makes a 12-year-old determined to be "straight." With their own vulnerabilities and stresses, these children have developed ways of coping with the moment and, for some, with their futures.

"Coping" means to contend with, or struggle with, but in the literature of "risk" research, it has come to mean a positive, functional response to adversities. Coping offspring are those who have overcome the odds. "Stress-resistant" children (Garmezy, 1985; Rutter, 1985), "Superkids" (Kaufman, Gruenbaum, Cohler, & Gamer, 1979), and "invulnerable" children (Anthony & Cohler, 1987) have been studied to identify child qualities and environmental conditions that help to explain the positive coping. But, as Murphy and Moriarty (1976) make the case, all children, or most all, not only those who succeed, are making "coping" or protective efforts throughout their development. Ideally we should trace their serial cognitive and behavioral "contending" with acute and chronic stresses in their lives with depressed parents.

As the literature speaks of children's coping "strategies," it has the sound of behavior planfully followed and acknowledged by the child. But coping undoubtedly involves much that the child is not aware of or cannot acknowledge. The two sisters who have taken care of each other from early childhood may or may not describe this dependency as their coping strategy. On the other hand, the attic retreat will probably be a lasting memory for the boy who used it. Then there are devious ways of coping. An ill mother victimizes her younger child. The older sibling gets her

Table 13.2 *Children's methods of coping*
(% of children of depressed mothers)

Coping method	Younger siblings		Older siblings	
	Boys	Girls	Boys	Girls
Care giving–emotional	24.2	11.4	24.0	18.0
Care giving–instrumental	15.2	14.3	32.0	35.9
Avoiding, escaping temporarily	60.6	45.7	64.0	59.0
Leaving family	9.1	8.6	4.0	23.1
Engaging in physical activity	30.3	5.7	44.0	7.7
Finding substitute relationship	51.5	68.6	48.0	66.7
Achieving	24.2	42.9	52.0	38.5
Being a "good" person	24.2	45.7	36.0	30.8
Keeping feelings inside	27.3	34.3	32.0	43.6
Intellectualizing, turning to religion	12.1	8.6	20.0	15.4
Blaming self	15.1	8.6	0.0	5.1
Making artistic expression	6.1	17.1	28.0	35.9

mother's limited affection by siding with her mother in unmerciful criticism of her sister. This behavior is not likely to be a reported strategy.

Lacking knowledge of the coping aspect of offspring development, research on the effects of maternal depression on children is without an important consequence in the lives of offspring. This information is difficult to obtain, and our information on coping is limited.

Late in the children's development, we asked them what they did when things were going badly at home. By this time, the children of ill mothers were well aware of the study purposes, and most talked about their families. The questioning called for children's descriptions of specific instances and actions, not a generalization. A second data source was the log record. Descriptions from the two sources were coded, as represented in Table 13.2.

Children's responses reveal a wide variety of reactions, multiple methods used by most of the children, and similarity of methods across gender and age. Care giving to the depressed mother, in the sense of providing emotional support or comfort, and care giving in the instrumental sense of taking on household or child care responsibilities are described equally often by boys and girls. However; in an earlier report on the care giving of boys and girls (Radke-Yarrow & Brown, 1993), the nature of care giving appears to be somewhat gender-linked; that is, care giving by boys at these ages has the sound of an "executive" function: "I'm the man of the house." "They come to me for help." "I'm the good brother." Emotional care giving appears in both boys and girls.

Children also make explicit attempts to avoid, both physically and psychologically, the problems of the family. For a few children, this means taking action to move out of the family.

Only in describing their immediate reactions to traumatic events in the family are there clear gender differences. Boys get out of the house, beyond the sounds, and throw balls at the garage door or shoot baskets. Fewer girls, similarly seeking escape in activity, may walk the dog. Equally often boys and girls describe what they cannot escape, namely, physical tension.

Boys and girls turn equally to a substitute relationship as a means of dealing with stressors (friend, sibling, other relative, teacher, therapist, pet). Some children are fortunate in having a supportive person find them.

Children also turn to themselves and invest in goals or activities that bring personal satisfaction – high academic achievement, leading a "good" life, artistic expression. Rumination about mother's illness, wondering about its causes, and agonizing and worrying about their own role are frequent descriptions by both boys and girls, indicating draining coping efforts.

One might ask about the success of these varied responses to stress, and about the temperament qualities of children responding in various ways. The data are not adequate to answer these questions, however, because many of the children report multiple kinds of responses, and children may, in many instances, not recognize certain behaviors as patterns of coping. Nevertheless, the data are revealing of children's efforts in dealing with stress. They also demonstrate a level of children's awareness concerning some of the effects of parental psychopathology on themselves. This cognitive–affective area is much in need of study.

We do not learn from the children's responses the underlying feelings in their varied reactions. Is "being good" expressing self-blame, or is it fear of becoming like mother, or is it a way of avoiding mother's anger or of getting some positive attention? Is the care giving an empathic devotion, or is it motivated by anxiety? How does the child's understanding of mother's behavior as illness influence reactions?

Answers to these questions can come only from intimate knowledge of the children's behavior over an extended time and knowledge of their cognitive constructions about themselves and the interpersonal family world they have experienced. Answers are very relevant for planning interventions that are beneficial to children.

SIBLING DEVELOPMENT

Throughout the study, the individual child has been the unit, and siblings have been treated as two separate samples of offspring. We have not compared sibling pairs. The conceptualization of individual development as determined by the interaction of systems within the individual and systems within the family environment applies to each sibling, making the determinants of each sibling's development unique. Therefore, we would not expect to find a single explanatory principle or process to account for sibling similarities and differences. Indeed, we did not as we examined the development of siblings.

Information in this study permitted comparisons of sibling pairs on variables of person (intelligence, gender, temperament) and variables of parental treatment. These person variables do not explain sibling pairs who are alike or those who are different in development. We reach a similar conclusion from examination of parental treatment (see Table 13.3) and sibling outcomes. Only one symptom variable of the mother, negativity–anger, which has appeared repeatedly in predictions of individual children's devel-

Table 13.3 *Outcome diagnoses of sibling pairs in families of depressed mothers in relation to parental treatment (% of sibling pairs)*

	Outcomes of sibling pairs		
Parenting of siblings	Both with current problems ($n = 27$)	Both no problem ($n = 10$)	One sibling no problem, other recurrent ($n = 27$)
Mother angry–irritable	55.6	10.0	37.0[a]
Mother unavailable			
to both	14.8	0.0	0.0
to one child	18.5	0.0	14.8
Father provides some nurturance			
to both	51.9	30.0	44.4
to one child	7.4	20.0	18.5
Father rejects one child	14.8	30.0	40.7
Mother identifies child with her illness			
both	7.4	10.0	22.2
one child	44.4	20.0	14.8
Mother "uses" child			
both	7.4	0.0	7.4
one child	33.3	0.0	37.0

[a]With $p<.05$; all other comparisons of outcomes are nonsignificant.

163

opment, significantly increases the probability of similarity in sibling outcomes. Mother's negativity increases the frequency of psychopathology in both siblings.

Sibling pairs in roughly half of the families are similar in their problematic or nonproblematic status at T3,4, regardless of maternal diagnosis (50%, 62%, and 53% in families of bipolar, unipolar, and well mothers, respectively). A more defining comparison is similarity with respect to recurrent problems. Similarity in sibling pairs is 50% in families of unipolar mothers. It drops sharply to 27% in families of bipolar mothers, and to 7% in families of well mothers.

Ten sibling pairs with unipolar mothers have lifelong problems of depression and/or disruptive disorders. For these pairs, mothering themes, early and throughout childhood, differ for six of the ten pairs and are similar for four of the pairs.

Development of, or escape from, psychopathology by different children in the family, in our opinion, is best understood in terms of the developmental course of each child, formed by multiple processes. Siblings may have the same outcome of psychopathology, but the sources and routes to this outcome may be very different. Siblings may have different outcomes, yet have had many common experiences relating to mother's depression, interacting with the child's attributes, relationships, and experiences.

SUMMARY

The child emerges in our data as a proven contributor to his or her own course of development. This contribution is often through reciprocal processes. The individual children in our case descriptions illustrate child effects on environment and reciprocal child–environment effects. In chapter 5, Jenny, a very shy little girl, and her very needy and dependent depressed mother form a synchronous neediness that eventuates in serious problems. The functioning of family B in chapter 9 is almost in the hands of the angry, hostile children. Their two dysfunctional parents are overwhelmed. Adam's explosiveness (in this chapter), combined with his acting out and yelling mother, bring out their shared detrimental characteristics.

The larger question for theory and research is how best to conceptualize the caregiver–child dyad and make it the basic unit in investigating developmental processes, whether normal or psychopathological. Investigation of the mother–child dyad with the interacting attributes, behavior styles, and needs of each member of the dyad has been a step toward identifying processes in psychopathological development.

14

COMMON AND DIVERSE PATHWAYS, MECHANISMS, AND OUTCOMES

How do connections in children's patterns of behavior come about in the course of development, and *how* do linkages between parents' and children's psychopathologies develop? Rutter (1989b) has succinctly summarized the challenges in these questions, finding "unifying principles in the mechanisms underlying the diverse pathways from childhood to adult life . . . in personal terms and in the context of possible person–environment interactions" (p. 46). The questions do not set the usual goal of finding a best predictor. They indicate the diverse and multidetermined nature of individual development (Sroufe, 1979; Sroufe & Jacobvitz, 1989), including individual psychopathological development. Hence, the objective is to find commonalities and orderliness in the diversity. We now look to the collective findings from this study to examine what we have learned that is relevant to the challenges of these "how" questions.

First we examine extreme subgroups of families of depressed mothers. With an additive approach, we find families that are homogeneous at extremes with respect to person or environmental variables. Do they confirm the associations reported for the total group, and what more do they tell us? Our second focus is on offspring who are homogeneous in outcome – who are depressed. Do their behavioral and environmental histories identify patterns of factors that are specific risks for depression? Third, many variables and patterns of variables have been identified that are predictive of offspring development, and that suggest mechanisms influencing development. We bring these findings together to examine them for principles or generalizations regarding mechanisms of influence.

EXTREME SUBGROUPS – HIGH AND LOW IN RISK

The variables used to define the extreme groups are those which, singly, relate to offspring problems. Homogeneity is in the lifetime characteristics of the group.

Extremes in Environment

Extreme environmental risk is defined as a pattern of the mother's early and continuing impaired relationships with the child, combined with the father's dysfunction and/or rejection of the child, and family-wide high stress over time. (Many families, of course, are not very different from these concentrated risk qualities.)

Four younger siblings and six older siblings are classified in this "most risk" environment. At the end-point assessment, eight of the 10 children have a diagnosis of depression; seven have co-morbid conduct problems. Nine have difficulties in school and/or with peers. This group is a notch above the total sample in extent of problems and specifically depression, but this summation of environmental factors alone does not bring perfect prediction, and is nonspecific with regard to mechanisms.

The opposite extreme – the absence of these risks – defines the environments of four younger and two older children. None of these children has a diagnosis of depression at end-point assessment, but three have other diagnoses. All but one of the children are functioning well in school and with peers. Although these low-risk conditions do not fully protect the children, the record is better than that of the total sample, and it is very different from the opposite environmental extreme.

Extremes in Offspring Outcomes

To be in the most disturbed group of offspring requires a diagnosis of depression, with or without additional diagnoses, unsuccessful academic and behavioral performance in school, poor peer

167

relationships, and negative self-attitudes. Five children fit this dismal configuration.

Without exception, their families present a solid picture of multiple family risks: The mothers have low scores in functioning, have personality disorders, and are symptomatic in behavior with the child. The fathers are feared for their violent outbursts. Fathers are also not supportive in family relationships. High stress ratings across time characterize the families.

The match is 100%. But before it is interpreted in terms of additive risks residing solely in the family or parent, two additional facts are relevant: All of the children were diagnosed with disruptive–oppositional disorders in *early childhood*, and all but one of the children have a problem temperament, assessed in the early years. From the longitudinal picture of pervasive and lifelong person and environmental stresses, we infer a process of negative reciprocal interactions promoting offspring problems.

The fourth extreme group is composed of children who are without a diagnosis and are dealing competently with life (14 younger and 8 older children). The mothering they have experienced during most of childhood has been responsible and generally sensitive, although more than half of the mothers were functionally impaired by their illness when the study began. Only 14% are so rated at T3 evaluations. When, in earlier years, the mother was symptomatic, the father, in all cases, provided nurturance and care for the children. This is not a group in which children with problem temperaments have symptomatic mothers. Recurrent problems are not characteristic of these children, and family stress is moderately low. This is a success story, although open to various interpretations. Does credit go to the father's protective role, the mother's improved functioning, the child's less difficult behavior in the family, the child's less inherent vulnerability?

One family does not fit the profile of this subgroup. The family has been disastrously dysfunctional. The mother has had severely impairing episodes of depression; the father has been alcoholic; older siblings in the family have been violently disruptive and destructive, and have been temporarily hospitalized. However, for this family, there has been a dramatic turning point. At a most critical time in their lives, the mother's desperate behavior (she disappeared) brought the church community into active intervention with mother, father, and children. These interventions on many fronts appear to have been the keys to the successful functioning of the two children in our study, at least in this period in which conditions in the family have improved so dramatically. Such turning points, and such unpredictable "saving" events, were rarely observed in the families.

The data on extreme groups convincingly demonstrate that psychopathology "goes with" environmental risks. But, environments, even in the extreme, do not act uniformly on all children, and, by themselves, are not sufficient to explain outcomes. Child characteristics enter into the environment-to-offspring outcome processes.

DEPRESSED CHILDREN OF DEPRESSED MOTHERS

Depressed children now come under close examination. At the end point of assessments, 34% of the younger siblings and 53% of the older siblings have a diagnosis of depression (dysthymia or major depression). (Depression at T3,4 is, of course, an approximate end point. Depression may develop later in the lives of these offspring. The diagnoses of anxiety, disruptive disorders, and depression are not absolutely distinct entities; one problem expression may evolve into another.)

Our explorations take us to (1) follow-back comparisons of the offspring who are depressed with the offspring who have other outcomes, (2) follow-backs of depressed offspring who differ in their symptomatology, and (3) examination of longitudinal patterns of variables predictive of depression.

Developmental Histories of Offspring Classified by Outcome Diagnosis

We are interested in learning whether depressed children differ in any "historical" way from the children who have other diagnoses or no problems. Outcome classifications follow the patterns of problems observed in chapter 7: depression (D), depression and externalizing problems (D+Ext), anxiety, anxiety and externalizing problems, and no problems. Other internalizing disorders, such as somatic problems, may exist with depression and anxiety (see Table 14.1).

We see that depressed children (combining D and D+Ext) do not have a history of earlier behavior or environmental variables that consistently distinguishes them from children with other diagnoses, not on a variable-by-variable comparison. None of the other problem outcomes has a distinct developmental profile. Descriptively, the childhood parenting environment (rows 4, 5, and 6) appears to be somewhat more positive for the children with internalizing problems only (columns 1 and 4) than for children with externalizing problems (columns 2 and 3).

The findings are open to various interpretations. Perhaps all of the diagnoses are expressive of the same underlying disturbance. Perhaps we have compared outcomes on the wrong precursor conditions.

Developmental Histories in Relation to Differences within the Diagnosis of Depression

There is heterogeneity within the diagnosis of depression – children with depression only, children with depression and externalizing problems, children who have had major depressive episodes, and children who are showing signs of bipolar illness.

Depression Alone and Depression with Externalizing Disorders. Are these two patterns of problems different manifestations of the same disorder? Are they separate disorders with separate etiologies and prognoses? Caron and Rutter (1991) have posed these questions. The paths of development and the histories of family and parenting experiences should shed light on these questions.

Children who are later diagnosed as D and those diagnosed as

D+Ext are different very early in their histories. Before eight years, problems of disruptive behavior and depression are more frequent in the D+Ext children, whereas anxiety is more characteristic of the D children. Problematic temperament characteristics appear more often in the D+Ext children, and with very high frequency (75% of the younger and 65% of the older siblings). Problematic temperaments in the D children tend to be "low in pleasant sociability" rather than "difficult." The two groups of children do not differ in shyness.

Differences between D and D+Ext children continue through childhood in their daily functioning. More D+Ext than D children have troubles in school and with peers (chapter 6). However, recurrent psychiatric problems are present in almost all of the children in both groups. It is interesting that in children's professed methods of coping with their mother's illness (chapter 13), striving to be "good" is the way of 69% of the D children and only 19% of the D+Ext children.

Have these "different" children grown up in contexts that also differ? In the earliest years (1½ to 3½), qualities of mothering do not differ for D and D+Ext children. In childhood, the frequency of negatively symptomatic mothers does not differ. But we must recall the differences in temperament that D and D+Ext children bring to depressed mother and families. Putting mother and child qualities into dyadic compositions, we find a symptomatic mother paired with a child of problem temperament in 50% and 35% of the younger and older D+Ext children, respectively; in 29% and 0% of the D children.

Mothers of D+Ext children are rated less responsible throughout childhood. Also, family environment has harsher edges for these children. They experience explicit rejection from mother, father, siblings, and peers significantly more often than do the children with depression alone.

Thus, in behavioral histories and childhood environments, D depressed offspring and the D + Ext depressed offspring are different. Caron and Rutter proposed that depression with externalizing problems might be the result of different and independent

Table 14.1 *Offspring diagnoses in relation to family environment and child characteristics* (% of offspring)

Developmental history	Diagnoses of younger siblings					Diagnoses of older siblings				
	Depression only	Depression and externalizing problems	Anxiety and externalizing problems	Anxiety and/or other internalizing problems	No diagnosis	Depression only	Depression and externalizing problems	Anxiety and externalizing problems	Anxiety and/or other internalizing problems	No diagnosis
n	7	16	12	13	16	14	20	6	13	9
Environment										
First 3 years										
Symptomatic mothering	43	50	75	31	38					
Unsuccessful regulation	67	53	75	17	40					
Secure attachment	71	69	33	69	40					
Childhood years										
Negative mothering	43	56	67	31	19	43	50	83	31	0
Not responsible mothering	14	25	25	0	0	0	30	33	0	0
Rejection	29	50	33	31	13	36	60	67	54	0

Mother personality disorder	83	73	58	46	40	54	79	67	50	44
High interpersonal family stress	67	63	27	54	38	57	60	33	64	11
Child characteristics										
Problem temperament	57	75	75	39	38	14	65	33	69	78
Early disruptive problems	29	50	67	8	13	43	65	67	31	33
Early depressive problems	14	44	67	46	25	57	70	50	62	22
Early anxiety problems	71	44	67	8	25	71	55	17	39	22
Recurrent problems	71	94	100	46	19	79	100	83	92	11
Poor school performance	14	38	42	8	0	7	40	33	8	11
Poor peer relationships	43	56	42	15	13	36	70	50	31	11

Note: Diagnosis of only disruptive problems appears in four younger and two older siblings. They are not represented in the table.

risk factors operating for each disorder. They suggested environmental variables, such as family stress, as mediating factors in disruptive problems, and genetic factors as mediating depression.

Our finding of more aversive parenting for the children with comorbid problems is in line with the hypothesis regarding externalizing behavior having roots in environmental stresses. However, environmental stresses originating in dyadic incompatibilities have significant child components. Temperament characteristics are not environmental variables, although in dyadic patterns, they create different environments. Further, as reported earlier, a secure attachment relationship (not easily classified as environmental or genetic) is significantly associated with depression later in development, and, when combined with some parenting behavioral risks, secure attachment is associated also with disruptive problems. Thus, specific and different environmental conditions *from different origins* contribute to both depressive and disruptive problems. Mediating factors are not neatly divided.

Offspring with Major Depression. One or more major depressive episodes have occurred in 22 of the children. Among the older siblings, 4, 10, and 3 children, and among the younger siblings, 1, 3, and 1 of the children of bipolar, unipolar, and well mothers, respectively, have had a major episode. The first major episodes occurred in the children of bipolar and well mothers between 8 and 19 years; in the children of unipolar mothers between 8 and 19 years. Of the children with major episodes, 80% have comorbid outcomes. Of the children with major episodes, 73% are girls. The parenting histories of these early-onset children do not differ in any consistent ways from the parenting histories of the other depressed children.

Offspring with Hypomanic Episodes. No child is diagnosed manic or manic–depressive, but seven meet criteria for Bipolar II disorder (DSM-IV criteria), as diagnosed by the DICA. All of these children (6 older and 1 younger sibling) have had major depressive episodes and hypomanic episodes. Surprisingly, six are children of unipolar depressed mothers; one is a child of a well mother. All are girls.

Signs of Bipolar Illness. Because there is a long history of not-too-successful clinical attempts to identify early signs of bipolar illness in children and adolescents, we pursued, in more detail, early signs of bipolar illness.

Early signs of bipolar illness in children are variously reported in the literature. In rare cases, the classic symptoms of manic–depression have been described in 4- to 7-year-olds (e.g., Poznan-ski, Israel, & Grossman, 1984; Tomasson & Kuperman, 1990). Isaac (1991) suggests that bipolar illness in prepubertal and pubertal children may be quite common and may be underdiagnosed among the very-hard-to-diagnose and seriously problematic children. In adolescence, behavior characteristic of the adult-form manic–depression appears (review by Carlson, 1983).

A "variant" manic–depressive syndrome has been proposed by Davis (1979), for children 6 to 16, identified by problems of affective storms, hyperactivity, troubled interpersonal relationships, and family history of bipolar illness. Other investigators (Kuyler, Rosenthal, Igel, Dunner, & Fieve, 1980; Kestenbaum, 1982; Kron, Decina, Kestenbaum, Farber, Gargan, & Fieve, 1982; Akiskal, Downs, Jordan, Watson, Daugherty, & Pruitt, 1985; Klein & De-pue, 1985; LaRoche, Cheifetz, Lester, Schibuk, DiTommaso, & En-gelsmann, 1985) have designated possible indicators: irritability, aggressiveness, emotional lability, distractibility, increased psychomotor activity, psychomotor retardation, hypersomnia, insomnia, explosive anger, obsessionality, grandiosity. But it is clear that these behavioral signs are not unique to bipolar illness.

We used the full array of symptoms suggested in the literature to examine their presence in the children with a bipolar mother or another relative with bipolar illness, the children of unipolar mothers (without bipolar history), and the children of well parents. The symptoms that are significantly different in these groups are listed in Table 14.2. Only a few symptoms differentiate the groups, and not consistently at each assessment: namely, lack of

Table 14.2 Symptoms that differ significantly (p <.05) in children with bipolar, unipolar, and well family history

Age period	Symptom	Bipolar[a] Younger siblings	Bipolar[a] Older siblings	Unipolar Younger siblings	Unipolar Older siblings	Well Younger siblings	Well Older siblings
5–8 years	Lack of impulse control		27		9		3
	Frequent temper		87		59		60
	Insomnia	20		38		13	
	Rapid speech	38	17	65	9	23	0
8–11 years	Lack of impulse control		17		9		0
	Frequent temper	53		50		20	
	Psychomotor agitation	53	20	38		20	
	Poor concentration	24		35	6	10	3
11–15 years	Rapid speech		43	53			20
	Psychomotor agitation		23	38			10
	Psychomotor retardation		23	32			7
	Poor concentration		40	27			13

[a]Includes children with a bipolar mother and four younger and four older children of unipolar depressed mothers with relatives with bipolar illness.

impulse control, frequent temper, rapid speech, psychomotor agitation, and poor concentration.

The picture for the seven hypomanic children is sleep problems (100%), temper tantrums (86%), psychomotor problems (57%), and attention deficit/hyperactivity (57%) in the prepubertal years. Lack of impulse control (71%), pressured speech (86%), and racing thoughts (43%) appear in early adolescence.

We must conclude that our data do not help identify clear patterns of bipolar signs in the developmental histories. Even with this conclusion, however, in clinical judgment, bipolar expression is predicted for several children.

Further Predictors of Depression

In further exploration of possible factors leading to the expression of depression, we reassembled the variants in depression as a single diagnosis, bringing into consideration a genetic indicator and a longitudinal analysis of the depressed mother–child relationship.

An Index of Genetic Vulnerability in Relation to Offspring Depression. The very best of data sets, poised to predict depression, would have information on the child's genetic vulnerability, as well as on the environmental variables, but the appropriate genetic information is not yet available. One could then ask how environmental risks of given kinds, at given developmental periods, affect or are affected by the genetic vulnerability.

Since the mother's age at the onset of her depression has been interpreted as a possible indicator of genetic vulnerability (Weissman, Wickramaratne, Merikangas, Leckman, Prusoff, Caruso, Kidd, & Gammon, 1984), we asked whether offspring of mothers with early onset are more vulnerable to the environmental risks posed by the mother–child relationship than offspring of mothers with later onset. Onset before 19 years of age (the mean for our mothers) was considered early. For the younger siblings, we chose presence or absence of angry–irritable and enmeshing mothering (measured in the early years), and for the older siblings the child-

177

hood history of angry, denigrating mothering, as the environmental risks.

Among the younger children, the presence of both presumed genetic vulnerability and symptomatic mothering did not affect the appearance of depression (range from 31% to 38% for the various combinations of early onset and environmental risks). However, among the older siblings, with the combination of vulnerability and chronic maternal anger and irritability, 71% of the children are depressed at outcome, compared with 47%, 50%, and 48% of the children with only one or neither of the risks. The difference, although not statistically significant ($p = .12$), suggests analyses to be pursued with stronger genetic indicators and with varied environmental risks.

Attachment Pattern and Later Depression. The relation of offspring depression to attachment prompted a search for the patterns of conditions that connect early experience with a depressed mother and children's subsequent development.

Reviewing the findings reported in chapter 12, we see that the attachment pattern is unrelated to later disorders in the children of well mothers, but, with depressed mothers, later depressive disorders are more frequent when the relationship has been secure than when it has been insecure. With asymptomatic depressed mothers, secure attachment is protective with respect to later disruptive disorders and anxiety; it is not protective with respect to children's later depression. With symptomatic mothers, secure attachment brings even greater risk for later problems. Thus, the function of attachment changes, depending on the nature of the affective transactions between mother and child.

Consider the affective interchanges between the depressed mother and her child. Mother's dysregulated affect (irritability and anger, intense contact and anxious affection, sadness, affectlessness, inaccessibility, and also inseparability) engages the child in complex, intense, and confusing communications. The potential cognitive–affective consequences would appear to be many. Can we assume that the child very early learns some of these patterns as his/her own? Is the affective intensity rewarding or overwhelming? Do mother's mixed affective messages contribute to dysregulation in the child? The data suggest all of these consequences but not uniformly for all children.

To try to obtain insight into processes intervening between these early affective experiences and the child's later psychiatric status, we traced forward the environment and behavior of the securely attached children, grouping them according to their outcomes.

Among the children who later become depressed, two subgroups with quite different pathways are distinguishable. Ten of the children are securely attached to enmeshing and/or negative, irritable mothers and/or mothers with personality disorders. Closeness to mothers is apparently rewarding and supportive: Seven of the children are without problems in early years. None is showing depressive affect. Temperament characteristics vary.

A major change takes place in the mother–child relationship in middle or later childhood that is best summarized as a critical loss for the child. Very difficult relationships develop, for varied reasons: There is a change for the worse in mother's depression, with increased negativity and outright rejection. ("My little doll" becomes someone "I feel sometimes I could kill.") For other mother and child pairs, developmental autonomy needs and conflicts in the child and continuing needy dependency by the mother are incompatible. Both participants or the child alone become hostile and rejecting. In this sequence of relationships, the child's loss is continuous.

A second subgroup ($n = 6$) whose later diagnosis is depression has a different early-to-later connectedness. These children are in a close relationship with a symptomatic mother. All of the children have problem temperaments. Unlike the children in the previous group, these children are showing substantial depressive affect by six years, and their problems continue. They appear very early to be especially vulnerable children.

Securely attached children have other than depression as outcomes. Secure attachments with a later diagnosis of anxiety or disruptive problems do not have clear patterns of sequential conditions. On the other hand, the secure children with no problems

179

at the end of childhood do present a common path. Six of the seven are growing up relatively problem-free with an asymptomatic mother. None of the mothers has a personality disorder.

Insecure attachment, a symptomatic mother, and a child of problematic temperament define another group of children ($n = 7$) who become depressed. Theirs is a turbulent childhood, in relationships with the mother and in recurrent problems. All of the mothers have personality disorders. They are angry or uninvolved. All but one of the children have problem temperaments.

An interesting contrasting sequence appears with insecure attachments to a symptomatic mother. Six children in these double-risk contexts develop few problems. This course requires more study, but we speculate that the aversive maternal conditions activate protective processes in the children, at least at the behavioral level. Insecure attachments may be minimizing exposure to the mother, thereby, in one sense, minimizing the maternal risk. This is not a new idea. Anthony and Cohler (1987) suggest that under some circumstances, such as parental psychopathology, insecure attachment or distance from the mother might have a protective function.

Observations of these children illustrate their protective strategies, especially the children of mothers with bipolar illness. The children ignore the mother, separate from the mother without apparent distress, and interact with pleasure with other adults. In like fashion, siblings form partnerships, as if not needing the mother, perhaps as a means of lessening stress.

Summary. The data on the longitudinal pathways are descriptive. They leave many gaps to be filled in on the mother–child pairs. Their replicability needs to be established. Nevertheless, with certainty, the subgroup patterns bring out the reality of diverse person–environment interactions in paths toward maturity.

The subgroups show also that the relative importance of person factors and environmental factors in determining course of development varies in different patterns. Such a difference is apparent in the two subgroups of securely attached children whose outcome is depression. The children who were exhibiting depressive

180

affects before six years and recurrently thereafter seemed to be a strongly influential force in the developmental trajectory. In contrast, in the subgroup of initially well-functioning children who experienced later loss of their positive mother–child relationship, the environment (mother's behavior) appears to have considerable influence. Such varied "weights" of person and environmental variables add further heterogeneity to transmission processes.

MECHANISMS UNDERLYING DEPRESSED MOTHER-TO-OFFSPRING LINKAGES

Many associations have appeared between parent psychopathology (and its correlates) and offspring disorders. Have these findings paved the way for the essential move beyond associations to underlying mechanisms, and, further, do the data meet the challenge of revealing principles in the mechanisms that underlie parent–offspring linkage?

A Review of Linkages

As a first step toward these objectives, we review the associations we have found, in the form of an inventory. There are first the differences in offspring problems associated with maternal diagnoses and stage of development:

1. At each age, children of depressed mothers have higher rates of psychiatric and psychosocial problems than children of well mothers.

2. Recurrent problems especially are more prevalent in the offspring of depressed mothers.

3. In the offspring of depressed mothers, problems are significantly present in the prepubertal years. Prepubertal depressive problems are very likely to continue into later years.

181

4. Developmental stage and psychiatric disorders are differently related in offspring of unipolar and bipolar mothers.

5. Problems of depression develop earliest and increase most rapidly in children of unipolar mothers.

Qualities of mother's illness influence rates of offspring problems:

6. Increased rates of problems are associated with depressed mothers' inability to function in essential and routine roles, and with depressed mothers' personality disorders.

The family context of stress is related to offspring problems:

7. Family-wide pervasive cumulative stress is modestly related to offspring problems.

8. High levels of family-wide stress combined with mothers' depression-related dysfunction are related to increased problems of depression in the adolescent years.

Depressed mothering characteristics are associated with high rates of offspring problems.

9. Depressed and well mothers' failure in helping the child to achieve self-regulation in the early years is associated with later offspring problems.

10. Highest rates of offspring problems are associated with depressed mothering that is characterized by anger and irritability and/or enmeshing dependency (often combined).

11. Gender differences in disruptive disorders interact with age and maternal diagnosis. Girls of depressed mothers have high rates of these disorders.

The depressed mother–child relationship in the early years and throughout childhood is a key influence in offspring development.

12. The interaction of maternal depression and the early attachment pattern enters complexly into offspring development.

13. The sequence of mother–child relationships over time (con-

tinuity and change) is an important influence on offspring outcomes.

The child is a significant contributor to his/her own course of development.

14. Mother–child dyads comprised of a child with a problem temperament and an affectively symptomatic mother are associated with high rates of disorder in the offspring.

15. In problematic dyads, negative properties of mother and child, through reciprocal influences, tend to escalate over time.

16. Specific configurations of mother's affectively symptomatic behavior, mother–child relationship, and family stress involving continuing or repeated risk conditions, acting together, are especially influential in offspring psychopathology.

Unifying Principles

An inventory does not provide an integrative framework for the findings although it reinforces the conception of behavior as multidetermined. However, with the inventory and from the perspective of developmental theory, several unifying principles in the processes of transmission of psychopathology are visible.

1. The transmission of psychopathology is especially promoted by patterns of depressed mother's behavior that impinge *directly* on the child by *interfering with fundamental developmental tasks and needs*. Interference begins early and continues. Maternal impairments that do significant developmental damage to offspring (a) strike at the child's development of self-regulation of behavior and affect, (b) destabilize long-term dependable security for child, (c) manipulate the child's autonomy and dependency needs, and (d) undermine positive attitudes regarding the self.

In other words, depressed mothers vary in the specific risks they bring to their children, but many of the risks that have significant consequences have in common the destructive interferences with basic developmental processes. Their children are thereby made particularly vulnerable to dysregulation and dysfunction across a wide swath of functioning.

2. A second principle in transmission draws on the view of behavior as embedded in multiple social environmental contexts. The "layers" of contexts that have been investigated in this study are the ambience of family relationships, the mother's behavior expressive of her illness, and the depressed mother's relationship with her child. It is the *consistency and pervasiveness of messages across these interrelated contexts* that increase offspring vulnerability. Networks of interdependent and repetitive conditions leave few escape routes and encourage maladaptive offspring behavior.

3. The *nature of the child* is a third significant determinant of how and how much parent psychopathology is transmitted to offspring. There are many unknowns regarding the role of inherent child properties in the mechanisms of transmission. Our data touch on only limited aspects of the child's nature, but the data are conclusive as to its importance, not alone, but in the company of environmental risk conditions.

In summary, although these principles underlying processes of transmission are drawn from the special case of parental depression and offspring development, we suggest that they are principles that are applicable, too, to the general case of parental influences on offspring development.

15

PREDICTION AND UNDERSTANDING OF DEVELOPMENT

"Will I only get worse like mom?" "All the craziness in our family! Are other families like mine?" "Do I have bipolar in me?" In their expectations and fears, transmission of mother's depression to offspring is a reality for these children. Our search into their lives and the lives of their families had as its goal to add to the understanding of the process.

IN BRIEF

The data revealed what these children knew and feared, that mother's depression can affect children's lives deeply and broadly. We learned much about the experiences of growing up with a depressed mother, the varied paths of development, and the factors that make a difference.

Evidence of offspring impairments appeared at each period of childhood. This finding does not convey the age-dependent differences in how mother's illness impacts on the child. The influential transactions are bound up with the child's capacities, needs, and behavioral requirements at different ages.

Across childhood and adolescence, mother's illness is conspicuously influential in the nature, frequency, and recurrence of offspring disorders. Again these outcomes represent the effects of diverse conditions and processes.

Links between maternal depression and offspring outcomes are best understood when we were able to identify sets of variables that in combination shaped the direction of the child's development. Such patterns of variables furnish the kinds of information that allow inferences regarding the mechanisms involved in common and diverse outcomes.

ISSUES FOR FURTHER STUDIES OF CHILDREN OF DEPRESSED PARENTS

Informal data from the parents and children in this study raise questions on a number of important substantive topics, and they furnish suggestive information. We comment on three questions: How does paternal depression influence offspring? What are the cognitive components of children's responses to parental psychopathology? How do societal attitudes regarding mental illness affect the children of depressed parents?

Depression Is Not Limited to Mothers

Although our families were selected on the basis of mother's diagnosis of depression, many of the fathers also were depressed (chapter 4). Although more women than men have diagnoses, there are many depressed men, and many depressed men who are fathers. Offspring research has greatly emphasized mothers in relation to offspring psychopathology. In future high-risk studies, contributions of husband and father to offspring problems deserve greater attention.

In this study, interviews with the mothers about the family's functioning provide a source of information on the fathers' behavior. Fathers' overt hostility, fits of anger, and physical violence, as well as fathers' complete inaccessibility were frequently described. Are children's predominant encounters with depressed fathers in hostile interactions? When both mother and father are depressed, how do they deal with each other's depression? How does the father's depression affect the child directly and through its influence on the mother? The probable trickle-down effects of father's pathology on the mother to the child should not result in underemphasizing the direct effects of the father's depression on the child. The strong influence of the early mother–child relationship raises an interesting question regarding transmission processes when the father is depressed. Are the effects of father's depression less environmentally mediated? Father's behavioral influences, we suspect, may have more impact in later childhood than in the early years. Father's outbursts in family life may "trigger" offspring problems more than lay the developmental groundwork for children's disorders.

How Do Children Comprehend Parental Depression?

With the emphasis on children's psychiatric diagnoses as the consequences of maternal illness, some of the psychological hardships that must be universal in offspring experience tend to go unnoticed and unstudied. Children's struggle to understand their symptomatic parents is such an area. It is a profoundly difficult and, no doubt, stressful task.

A parent is always a complex model. Generally, however, a reasonably stable behavioral repertoire becomes the expected behavior of the parent, based on the child's interactions with the parent, and on the child's observations of other parents. Children of symptomatic, depressed parents are faced with a difficult cognitive problem. They live with the parent's unpredictable behavior and also with the parent's behavior that is outside the boundaries of the "average" or expected in parental behavior. How is unpredictable and out-of-bounds behavior understood?

Although we did not systematically investigate children's interpretations of their parents' behavior, children's questions, actions, and emotions in the presence of parents' symptomatic behavior and their voiced expectations amply indicate their varied images of their parents. Fear, anger, compassion, shame, guilt, confusion, and hopelessness were all expressed.

A pair of siblings describe putting their arms around their mother and telling her about interesting things when she is "sad." A 2½-year-old stands "frozen" as his mother throws a temper tantrum at his sister. Then he retreats to the next room. A 12-year-old revolts when her mother is unable to function: She will no

187

longer do the cooking and laundry and get the younger children ready for school. Another child prays for her mother. A young teenager longs for her dead mother whom she sees as the person she is like. When a depressed father suddenly changes from a play partner to a silent, immobile, staring man stretched out on a chair, the children, grim-faced and "knowing," tiptoe around the father to mother, who encircles them in her arms.

The "tiptoes" reveal these children's expectations – they recognize a sequence of behavior in the father. The children who comfort their mother seem to be reflecting a history of care giving, and perhaps an understanding of mother's illness. The mother's tantrum behavior strikes fear into the toddler. In each instance, the children are sensitively aware of the parent's psychopathological behavior.

What are the children's cognitive constructions, and how do they influence children's management of their own stress? To accept or comprehend a definition of mother's behavior as illness is a peculiarly difficult task. When are children able to comprehend mental illness, and what kind of knowledge is protective? Is it too much to ask the impossible – to expect children also to integrate the mother's impairments with the turmoil in the family?

Children are given explanatory information from various sources. Mothers explain: "I'm manic–depressive. You have a 70% chance of being bipolar, like I am." Father shouts in anger, "You are just like your mother." A child in therapy finds "a load lifted" after his therapist explains his mother's illness. Going to visit his mother in the hospital brings the reality of "illness" into another child's perception, although he wavers: She is sick but "she can be fun."

We will better understand children's psychopathological development by having a grasp of these cognitive aspects. The importance of these data, unfortunately, is matched by difficulties in investigating children's comprehension.

The Social Meaning of Mental Illness

An understudied facet of offspring hardships is the presentation of parent, family, and self to the community and, especially, to peers. The stigma of mental illness varies in our society, depending on education, social class, and religion. There is little information on how this social threat affects children's adjustment. We know, anecdotally, that some children invest much in concealing mother's and/or father's strange behavior. They do not open their families to their friends. They do not want their mother to visit school. Less often (but it occurs), children take their parents' problems to support groups or persons (e.g., schools, clubs, priests). Children also report slurs and questions from peers and neighbors about their parents and themselves. At this intersection of family and community, there must be consequences for the children.

ISSUES OF THEORY AND METHODS

The toddler who dragged her blanket into the apartment and whimpered through the morning became the unhappy, isolated school child, followed by the turbulently disturbed and hospitalized teenager.

The 6-year-old who came to the study as an out-of-control and oppositional first-grader continued his disruptive pattern. By 10 years he had been drawn into a gang and had gotten into trouble with the law. By 14 years, he had become a studious high school student. After graduation, he was doing well on a job.

The competent 7-year-old took charge of her younger brother while their depressed mother painfully struggled through the research tasks. Three years later, this child again tried to deal with her parents' depression. This time, with her father present, she tried valiantly to brighten the gloomy situation by becoming a chatty "waitress" who served lunch to her family. At 16, she had made an attempt to hurt herself. She would not speak to her mother. She was too depressed to go to school.

These children contribute so very differently to the group findings on offspring outcomes. They represent different processes in development. With a closer look at them, we would see their different environmental and behavioral histories and their individual personal properties. We would, no doubt, locate these children in qualitatively distinct subgroups on the criteria we have investigated. They fit no easy generalization.

These children illustrate the complexity as well as the potential clarity that long-term longitudinal data introduce into questions of the effects of maternal depression on offspring and, in the broader perspective of developmental theory, into questions of parental influences on offspring.

We have seen that some understanding of these individual children is achieved, and some general developmental orderliness is revealed, by ferreting out patterns within the child and the environment that interactiviely have significance in development. This approach radically changes the research paradigm for parent–offspring studies.

A Revised Paradigm

Diverse influences and paths in individual development have always been expected, but, for the most part, diversity has remained "disorderly." Research, on the other hand, has pressed for "universals" in development, and in this process has to some extent squandered common wisdom.

A change from usual research operations in studies of parental influences on offspring could bring together the best of both perspectives by directing inquiry to the multiple "universals" that are determined by person–environment interactions. This shift affects the research design, data gathered, and methods of analysis.

In a revised paradigm, the child as a contributor to and modifier of parental influences renders inadequate research formulations of one-way influences of parent on child. The mutuality of influences requires analytic units that grasp this process. The parent–child relationship is one such unit. Also, because a relationship is longitudinal – with history and future expectations (Hinde, 1979) – it has the potential for pervasive influence on the offspring.

Second, a revised paradigm calls for an altered approach to environment as a research variable. When environment is conceptualized and measured in terms on a par with variables of person, it becomes possible to investigate mechanisms of person–environmental influences in individual behavior and development. It is not possible if environment is only estimated or is summarized in broad, static descriptions.

For the goal of arriving at an integrative framework for understanding individual development and for gaining insight into the adult from knowledge of a child's course, it goes without saying that development *in progress* is the essential medium for investigation of transmission processes.

The Variables

Many of the variables in this study are environmental variables; that is, they are the surroundings and interactions experienced by the child. However, these variables may, and do, have varied origins that have a bearing on their interpretation and, perhaps, also on their ultimate influence on the child. For example, a depressed mother's constant yelling at her child may have origins in her marital conflict. Or it may be a biologically anchored predisposition. Or it may be the normal parenting mode in her cultural group. Or it may be the symptoms of her depression. Or it may be all of these. It is doubtful that these differences in origin can be fully disentangled, but it is a reminder of the sometimes elusive distinctions of genetic, proximal environmental, and cultural elements in offspring development.

BEING A PARTICIPANT IN THE STUDY

This study, with our periodic examinations of the family's conditions, the mother's depression, and the children's functioning, was an intervention in the lives of the families. The families were faced with some self-appraisal and with increased awareness of their problems. At these times, they had, also, the clinician's "feedback." They had the ongoing availability of the clinician throughout the study, not for therapy, but for communication, advice, referral, and help in an emergency.

191

Most of these families struggle on their own. Parents, mainly the mothers, have or have had individual therapy, as have some of the fathers and children. Rarely have total families had coordinated help. Yet everyone in the family is involved in the stress and the risks. We wondered how much the inroads of parental depression on parenting functions are considered in the therapies that depressed mothers receive. For fathers' therapy, the question is equally relevant. The specific links identified in this study between parenting behavior and child problems might fruitfully be targeted interventions in therapy. We found that fathers rarely had help in dealing with the double problems of mother's depression and children's disorders.

Few of the families had social networks to which they could turn, or who were close enough to the family to feel free to intervene with caring help. Extended families were sometimes exceptions. The rare outside-family supports that existed had very positive effects. The supports often grew out of membership in religious groups. With these supports, the families survived crises and had sustaining help. The overall impression, however, is one of basic isolation of the individual family.

WHAT ARE THE EFFECTS OF MATERNAL DEPRESSION ON CHILDREN?

At the end point in our assessments, some children were without diagnosed problems or difficulties in social functioning, but few were untouched by their mother's depression. Many of the children entering adolescence and young adulthood had serious and multiple diagnoses, not only depression. They were doing poorly in significant areas of their lives and were fearfully anticipating the future. Some very depressed children were functioning successfully, even outstandingly, although their psychopathology and successful coping were in precarious balance. Overall, growing up as a child of a depressed parent is costly, through all of childhood and adolescence and to the threshold of adulthood.

192

REFERENCES

Achenbach, T., & Edelbrock, C. (1979). The child behavior profile: II: Boys aged 12–16 and girls aged 6–11 and 12–16. *Journal of Consulting and Clinical Psychology, 47,* 223–233.

Achenbach, T., & Edelbrock, C. (1983). *Manual for the child behavior check list and revised child behavior profile.* Burlington, VT: University of Vermont, Department of Psychology.

Ainsworth, M., Blehar, M., Waters, E., & Wall, D. (1978). *Patterns of attachment: A psychological study of the strange situation.* Hillsdale, NJ: Erlbaum.

Akiskal, H., Downs, J., Jordan, P., Watson, S., Daugherty, D., & Pruitt, D. (1985). Affective disorders in referred children and younger siblings of manic–depressives. *Archives of General Psychiatry, 42,* 966–1003.

Anthony, E., & Cohler, B. (1987). *The invulnerable child.* New York: Guilford Press.

Barker, R. (1968). *Ecological psychology: Concepts and methods for studying the environment of human behavior.* Stanford, CA: Stanford University Press.

Barker, R., Dembo, T., & Lewin, K. (1941). *Frustration and regression: An experiment with young children. University of Iowa Studies in Child Welfare, 18* (1).

Bartko, J., Strauss, J., & Carpenter, W. (1980). Selecting techniques for evaluating the reliability of psychiatric data: A report from the international pilot study of schizophrenia. In National Institute of Mental Health, Series GN No. 1, *Multivariate statistical methodologies used in the international pilot study of schizophrenia* (DHHS Publication No. (ADM) 80–630). Washington, DC: U.S. Government Printing Office.

Beardslee, W., Bemporad, J., Keller, M. B., & Klerman, G. L. (1983). Children of parents with a major affective disorder. *American Journal of Psychiatry, 140,* 825–832.

Bell, R. Q. (1968). A reinterpretation of the direction of effects in studies of socialization. *Psychological Review, 75,* 81–95.

Biederman, J., Rosenbaum, J., Hirshfeld, M., Faraone, S., Boldue, E., Gersten, M., Merringer, S., Kagen, J., Snidman, N., Resnick, S. (1990). Psychiatric correlates of behavioral inhibition in young children of parents with and without psychiatric disorders. *Archives of General Psychiatry,* *47,* 21–26.

Billings, A., & Moos, R. (1983) Comparisons of children of depressed and nondepressed parents: A social-environmental perspective. *Journal of Abnormal Child Psychology, 11* (4), 463–486.

Billings, A. G., & Moos, R. H. (1985). Children of parents with unipolar depression: A controlled 1-year follow-up. *Journal of Abnormal Child Psychology, 14,* 149–166.

Bronfenbrenner, U. (1979). *The ecology of human development: Experiments in nature and design.* Cambridge, MA: Harvard University Press.

Brown, G. W., & Harris, T. (1978). *Social origins of depression. A study of psychiatric disorder in women.* London: Tavistock.

Cairns, R. (1986). Phenomena lost: Issues in the study of development. In J. Valsiner (Ed.), *The individual subject and scientific psychology* (pp. 97–111). New York: Plenum Press.

Campbell, S. (1989). Developmental perspectives. In T. Ollendeck & M. Herson (Eds.), *Handbook of child psychopathology* (pp. 5–28). New York: Plenum Press.ʻ

Carlson, G. (1983). Bipolar affective disorders in childhood and adolescence. In D. Cantwell & G. Carlson (Eds.), *Affective disorders in childhood and adolescence. An update* (pp. 61–83). New York: SP Medical & Scientific Books.

Caron, C., & Rutter, M. (1991). Comorbidity in child psychopathology: Concepts, issues, and research strategies. *Journal of Child Psychology and Psychiatry, 2* (7), 1063–1080.

Cassidy, J., Marvin, R., & MacArthur Working Group on Attachment. (1987/89). *Attachment organization in three and four year olds. Coding guides.* Unpublished scoring manual.

Cicchetti, D., & Aber, J. L. (1986). Early precursors of later depression: An organizational perspective. In L. Lipsitt & Rovee-Collier (Eds.), *Advances in infant research* (Vol. 4, pp. 87–137). Norwood, NJ: Ablex.

Cohler, B. J., Grunebaum, H. U., Weiss, J. L., Gamer, E., & Gallant, D. H. (1977). Disturbance of attention among schizophrenic, depressed and well mothers and their young children. *Journal of Child Psychology and Psychiatry, 18,* 115–135.

Cohn, K., Matias, R., Tronick, E., Connell, D., & Lyons-Ruth, J. (1986). Face to face interactions of depressed mothers and their infants. In E. Tronick & T. Field (Eds.), *Maternal depression and infant disturbance* (pp. 31–46). San Francisco: Jossey-Bass.

Cooper, S. F., Leach, C., Storer, D., & Tonge, W. L. (1977). The children of psychiatric patients. *British Journal of Psychiatry, 131*, 514–522.

Cox, A. D., Puckering, C., Pound, A., & Mills, M. (1987). The impact of maternal depression in young people. *Journal of Child Psychology and Psychiatry, 28*, 917–928.

Coyne, J., & Downey, G. (1991). Social factors and psychopathology: Stress, social support and coping processes. In J. Spence (Ed.), *Annual Review of Psychology, 42*, 401–425.

Crittenden, P. (1988). Relationships at risk. In J. Belsky & T. Nesworski (Eds.), *Clinical implication of attachment theory* (pp. 136–174). Hillsdale, NY: Erlbaum.

Cummings, E., & Davis, P. (1994). Maternal depression and child development. *Journal of Child Psychology and Psychiatry, 35*(1), 73–112.

Cytryn, L., McKnew, D., Bartko, J., Lamour, M., & Hamovit, T. (1982). Offspring of patients with affective disorders. *Journal of American Academy of Child Psychiatry, 21*, 389–391.

Davenport, Y. B., Zahn-Waxler, C., Adland, M. L., & Mayfield, A. (1984). Early child-rearing practices in families with a manic–depressive parent. *American Journal of Psychiatry, 141*, 230–235.

Davis, R. (1979). Manic–depressive variant syndrome of childhood: A preliminary report. *American Journal of Psychiatry, 136*(5), 702–705.

Decina, P., Kestenbaum, C. J., Farber, S., Kron, L., Gargan, M., Sackheim, H. A., & Fieve, F. (1983). Clinical and psychological assessment of children of bipolar parents. *American Journal of Psychiatry, 140*, 548–553.

DeMulder, E., & Radke-Yarrow, M. (1991). Attachment with affectively ill and well mothers: Concurrent behavioral correlates. *Development and Developmental Psychopathology, 3*(2), 227–242.

DeMulder, E., Tarullo, L., Klimes-Dougan, B., Free, K., & Radke-Yarrow, M. (1995). Personality disorders of affectively ill mothers: Links to maternal behavior. *Journal of Personality Disorders, 9*(3), 199–212.

Derogatis, L. R. (1983). *SCL-90-R administration scoring and procedures manual II*. Minneapolis, MN: National Computer Systems Associations.

Diagnostic and Statistical Manual of Mental Disorders (3rd ed.; revised) (DSM III-R). Washington, D.C.: American Psychiatric Association, 1987.

Downey, G., & Coyne, J. C. (1990). Children of depressed parents: An integrative review. *Psychological Bulletin, 108*, 50–76.

Emery, R. E., Weintraub, S., & Neale, J. (1982). Effects of marital discord on the school behavior of children of schizophrenic, affective disordered, and normal parents. *Journal of Abnormal Child Psychology, 16*, 215–225.

REFERENCES

Endicott, J., Andreasen, N., & Spitzer, R. (1975). *Family history research diagnostic criteria.* New York: New York State Psychiatric Institute, Biometrics Research.

Endicott, J., Spitzer, R., Fleiss, J., & Cohen, J. (1976). The global assessment scale. *Archives of General Psychiatry, 33,* 766–771.

Engfer, A. (1988). The interrelatedness of marriage and the mother–child relationship. In R. Hinde & J. Stevenson-Hinde (Eds.), *Relationships within families* (pp. 104–118). Oxford: Clarendon Press.

Fendrich, M., Warner, V., & Weissman, M. (1990). Family risk factors, parental depression, and psychopathology in offspring. *Developmental Psychology, 26,* 40–50.

Field, T. (1984). Early interactions between infants and their postpartum depressed mothers. *Infant Behavior and Development, 7,* 517–522.

Forehand, R., Lautenschlager, G. J., Faust, J., & Graziano, W. G. (1986). Parent perceptions and parent–child interactions in clinic-referred children: A preliminary investigation of the effects of maternal depressive moods. *Behavior Research and Therapy, 24,* 73–75.

Gaensbauer, T. J., Harmon, R. J., Cytryn, L., & McKnew, D. H. (1984). Social and affective development in infants with a manic–depressive parent. *American Journal of Psychiatry, 141,* 223–229.

Garmezy, N. (1985). Stress-resistant children: The search for protective factors. In J. E. Stevenson (Ed.), *Aspects of current child psychiatry research.* Oxford, England: Pergamon Press.

Garrison, W., & Earls, F. (1985). Change and continuity in behaviour problems from the preschool period through school entry: An analysis of mother reports. In J. E. Stevenson (Ed.), *Recent Research in Developmental Psychopathology* (pp. 51–65). Oxford: Pergamon Press.

Gelfand, D., & Teti, D. (1990). The effects of maternal depression on children. *Clinical Psychology Review, 19,* 329–353.

Goodman, S. (1992). Understanding the effects of depressed mothers on their children. In E. F. Walker, R. H. Dworkin, & B. A. Cornblatt (Eds.), *Progress in experimental personality and psychopathology research* (Vol. 15). New York: Springer.

Goodman, S., & Brumley, H. (1990). Schizophrenic and depressed mothers: Relational deficits in parenting. *Developmental Psychology, 26* (1), 31–39.

Grizzle, J. E., Starmer, C. F., & Koch, G. G. (1969). Analysis of categorical data by linear models. *Biometrics, 25,* 489–505.

Grunebaum, H. U., Cohler, B. J., Kaufman, C., & Gallant, D. H. (1978).

Children of depressed and schizophrenic mothers. *Child Psychiatry and Human Development, 8,* 219–228.

Hammen, C. (1991). *Depression runs in families: The social context of risk and resilience in children of depressed mothers.* New York: Springer-Verlag.

Hammen, C., Adrian, C., Gordon, D., Burge, D., Jaenicke, C., & Hiroto, D. (1987a). Children of depressed mothers: Maternal strain and symptom predictors of dysfunction. *Journal of Abnormal Psychology, 96* 190–198.

Hammen, C., Gordon, D., Burge, D., Adrian, C., Jaenicke, C., & Hiroto, G. (1987b). Maternal affective disorders, illness, and stress: Risk for children's psychopathology. *American Journal of Psychiatry, 144,* 736–741.

Harder, D., Kokes, R., Fisher, L., & Strauss, J. (1980). Child competence and psychiatric risk. IV. Relationships of parent diagnostic classifications and parent psychopathology severity to child functioning. *Journal of Nervous and Mental Disease, 168,* 343–347.

Harter, S. (1979). The perceived competence scale for children. *Child Development, 58,* 87–97.

Herjanic, B., & Reich, W. (1982). Development of a structured psychiatric interview for children: Agreement between child and parent on individual symptoms. *Journal of Abnormal Child Psychology, 19*(3), 307–324.

Hinde, R. (1979). *Towards understanding relationships.* London: Academic Press.

Hinde, R. (1980). Family influences. In M. Rutter (Ed.), *Scientific foundations of developmental psychiatry* (pp. 47–66). London: Heinemann.

Hinde, R. (1988). Introduction. In R. Hinde & J. Stevenson-Hinde (Eds.), *Relationships within families: Mutual influences* (pp. 1–4). Oxford: Clarendon Press.

Hodges, K., Kline, J., Fitch, P., McKnew, D., & Cytryn, L. (1981). The child assessment schedule: A diagnostic interview for research and clinical use. *Catalog of Selected Documents in Psychology, 11,* 56.

Hops, H., Biglan, A., Sherman, L., Arthur, J., Friedman, L., & Osteen, V. (1987). Home observations of family interactions of depressed women. *Journal of Consulting and Clinical Psychology, 55*(3), 341–346.

Isaac, G. (1991). Bipolar disorder in prepubertal children in a special educational setting: Is it rare? *Journal of Clinical Psychiatry, 52,* 165–168.

Jaenicke, C., Hammen, C., Zupan, B., Hiroto, D., Gordon, D., Adrian, C.,

& Burge, D. (1987). Cognitive vulnerability in children at risk for depression. *Journal of Abnormal Child Psychology, 15,* 559–572.

Kagan, J. (1984). *The nature of the child.* New York: Basic Books.

Kagan, J., Resnick, J., Clark, C., Snidman, N., & Garcia-Coll, C. (1984). Behavioral inhibition to the unfamiliar. *Child Development, 55,* 2212–2225.

Kalbfleisch, J., & Prentice, R. (1980). *The statistical analysis of failure time data.* New York: John Wiley & Sons.

Kaufman, C., Grunebaum, H., Cohler, B., & Gamer, E. (1979). Superkids: Competent children of psychotic mothers. *American Journal of Psychiatry, 136*(11), 1398–1402.

Keller, M. B., Beardslee, W. R., Dorer, D. J., Lavori, P. W., Samuelson, H., & Klerman, G. R. (1986). Impact of severity and chronicity of parental affective illness on adaptive functioning and psychopathology in children. *Archives of General Psychiatry, 43,* 930–937.

Kestenbaum, C. J. (1982). Children and adolescents at risk for manic–depressive illness: Introduction and overview. *Psychiatry, 10,* 245–255.

Klein, D., Clark, D., Dansky, L., & Margolis, E. (1988). Dysthymia in the offspring of parents with primary unipolar affective disorder. *Journal of Abnormal Psychology, 94,* 115–127.

Klein, D., & Depue, R. (1985). Obsessional personality traits and risk for bipolar affective disorder: An offspring study. *Journal of Abnormal Psychology, 94*(3), 291–297.

Klein, D., Depue, R., & Slater, J. (1985). Cyclothymia in the adolescent offspring of parents with bipolar affective disorder. *Journal of Abnormal Psychology, 94*(2), 115–127.

Koch, A., Landis, J., Freeman, J., & Freeman, D. (1977). A general methodology for the analysis of experiments with repeated measurement of categorical data. *Biometrics, 33,* 133–158.

Kochanska, G. (1991). Patterns of inhibition to the unfamiliar in children of normal and affectively ill mothers. *Child Development, 62,* 250–263.

Kochanska, G., Kuczynski, L., Radke-Yarrow, M., & Welsh, J. D. (1987). Resolutions of control episodes between well and affectively ill mothers and their young child. *Journal of Abnormal Child Psychology, 15,* 441–456.

Kovacs, M. (1980). Rating scales to assess depression in school-aged children. *Acta Paedopsychiatria, 46,* 305–315.

Kron, L., Decina, P., Kestenbaum, C. J., Farber, S., Gargan, M.,& Fieve, R. (1982). The offspring of bipolar and manic–depressives: Clinical features. *Adolescent Psychiatry, 10,* 273–291.

Kuyler, P. L., Rosenthal, L., Igel, G., Dunner, D. L., & Fieve, R. R. (1980). Psychopathology among children of manic–depressive patients. *Biological Psychiatry, 15* (4), 589–597.

Landis, R., Heyman, E., & Koch, G. (1978). Average partial association in three-way contingency tables: A review and discussion of alternative tests. *International Statistical Review, 46,* 237–254.

LaRoche, C., Cheifetz, P., Lester, E. P., Schibuk, L., DiTommaso, E., & Engelsmann, F. (1985). Psychopathology in the offspring of parents with bipolar affective disorders. *Canadian Journal of Psychiatry, 30,* 337–343.

Ledingham, J., & Schwartzman, A. (1984). A 3 year follow-up of aggressive and withdrawn behavior in childhood: Preliminary findings. *Journal of Abnormal Child Psychology, 12,* 157–168.

Lee, C. M., & Gotlib, I. H. (1989). Maternal depression and child adjustment: A longitudinal analysis. *Journal of Abnormal Psychology, 98*(1), 78–85.

Lee, C., & Gotlib, I. (1991). Adjustment of children of depressed mothers at 20-month follow-up. *Journal of Abnormal Psychology, 100*(4), 473–477.

Lewin, K. (1931). Environmental forces in child behavior and development. In C. Murchison (Ed.), *A handbook of child psychology* (2nd ed.) (pp. 590–625). Worcester, MA: Clark University Press.

Lewin, K., Lippitt, R., & White, R. (1939). Patterns of aggressive behavior in experimentally created social climates. *Social Psychology, 10,* 271–299.

Lombroso, P., Pauls, D., & Leckman, J. (1995). Genetic mechanisms in childhood psychiatric disorders. In M. Hertzig & E. Farber (Eds.), *Annual progress in child psychiatry and child development* (pp. 171–205). New York: Brunner/Mazel.

Loranger, A. (1988). *Personality disorder examination (PDE) manual.* Yonkers, NY: DV Communications.

Luthar, S. (1991). Vulnerability and resilience: A study of high-risk adolescents. *Child Development, 62,* 600–616.

Magnusson, D., & Bergman, L. (1988). Individual and variable-based approaches to longitudinal research on early risk factors. In M. Rutter (Ed.), *Studies of psychosocial risk: The power of longitudinal data* (pp. 45–61). Cambridge: Cambridge University Press.

Masten, A., Garmezy, N., Tellegen, A., Pelligrini, D., Larkin, K., & Larsen, A. (1988). Competence and stress in school children: The moderating effects of individual and family qualities. *Journal of Child Psychology and Psychiatry, 29,* 745–764.

Murphy, L., & Moriarty, A. (1976). *Vulnerability, coping, and growth from infancy to adolescence.* New Haven, CT: Yale University Press.

Nolen-Hoeksema, S. (1987). Sex differences in unipolar depression: Evidence and theory. *Psychological Bulletin, 101*(2), 259–282.

Nurnberger, J., Goldin, L., & Gershon, E. (1986). Genetics of psychiatric disorders. In G. Winokur & P. Clayton (Eds.), *Medical basis of psychiatry* (pp. 486–521). Philadelphia: W. B. Saunders.

Orvaschel, H., Walsh-Allis, G., & Ye, W. (1988). Psychopathology in children of parents with recurrent depression. *Journal of Abnormal Child Psychology, 16*, 17–28.

Orvaschel, H., Weissman, M., & Kidd, K. (1980). The children of depressed parents; the childhood of depressed patients; depression in children. *Journal of Affective Disorders, 2*, 1–16.

Pellegrini, D. (1982). *Life stress interview: Events and chronic difficulties.* Unpublished manual. Washington, DC: Catholic University of America, Department of Psychology.

Poznanski, E., Israel, M., & Grossman, J. (1984). Hypomania in a four-year-old. *American Academy of Child Psychiatry, 23*(1), 105–110.

Radke-Yarrow, M. (1991). The individual and the environment in human behavioural development. In P. Bateson (Ed.), *The development and integration of behaviour: Essays in honour of Robert Hinde* (pp. 384–410). Cambridge: Cambridge University Press.

Radke-Yarrow, M., & Brown, E (1993). Resilience and vulnerability in children of multiple risk families. *Development and Psychopathology, 5*, 581–592.

Radke-Yarrow, M., Cummings, E., Kuczynski, L., Chapman, M. (1985). Patterns of attachment in two- and three-year-olds in normal families and families with parental depression. *Child Development, 56*, 884–893.

Radke-Yarrow, M., Nottelmann, E., Belmont, B., & Welsh, J. (1993). Affective interactions of depressed and nondepressed mothers and their children. *Journal of Abnormal Child Psychology, 21*(6), 683–695.

Radke-Yarrow, M., Nottelmann, E., Martinez, P., Fox, M., & Belmont, B. (1992). Young children of affectively ill parents: A longitudinal study of psychosocial development. *Journal of the American Academy of Child and Adolescent Psychiatry, 31*, 68–77.

Radke-Yarrow, M., & Sherman, T. L. (1990). Hard growing: Children who survive. In J. E. Rolf, A. Masten, D. Cicchetti, K. Nuechterlein, & S. Weintraub (Eds.), *Risk and protective factors in the development of psychopathology* (pp. 97–119). Cambridge: Cambridge University Press.

Reid, M., Landesman, S., Treder, R., & Jaccard, J. (1989). "My family and friends": 6- to 12-year-old children's perceptions of social support. *Child Development, 60*(4), 896–910.

Richman, N., Stevenson, J., & Graham, P. J. (1982). *Preschool to school: A behavioral study.* London: Academic Press.

Rutter, M. (1985). Resilience in the face of adversity: Protective factors and resistance to psychiatric disorder. *British Journal of Psychiatry, 147,* 598–611.

Rutter, M. (1988). Longitudinal data in the study of causal processes: Some uses and some pitfalls. In M. Rutter (Ed.), *Studies of psychosocial risk: The power of longitudinal data* (pp. 1–28). Cambridge: Cambridge University Press.

Rutter, M. (1989a). Isle of Wight revisited: Twenty-five years of child psychiatric epidemiology. *Journal of the American Academy of Child and Adolescent Psychiatry, 28*(5), 633–653.

Rutter, M. (1989b). Pathways from childhood to adult life. *Journal of Child Psychology and Psychiatry, 30*(1), 23–51.

Rutter, M. (1989c). Temperament: Conceptual issues and clinical implications. In G. Kohnstamm, J. Bates, & M. Rothbart (Eds.), *Temperament in childhood* (pp. 463–479). London: John Wiley & Sons.

Rutter, M. (1990). Commentary: Some focus and process considerations regarding the effects of parental depression on children. *Developmental Psychology, 26,* 60–67.

Rutter, M., MacDonald, H., Le Couteur, A., Harrington, R., Bolton, P., & Bailey, J. (1990). Genetic factors in child psychiatric disorders: Empirical findings. *Journal of Child Psychology and Psychiatry, 31*(1), 39–80.

Rutter, M., & Quinton, D. (1984). Parental psychiatric disorder: Effects on children. *Psychological Medicine, 14,* 855–880.

Rutter, M., & Shaffer, D. (1980). A step forward or back in terms of the classification of child psychiatric disorders. *American Academy of Child Psychiatry,* 371–394.

Sameroff, A., & Chandler, M. (1975). Reproductive risk and the continuum of care-taking causality. In F. D. Horowitz, M. Hetherington, S. Scarr-Salapatek, & G. Siegel (Eds.), *Review of child development research* (Vol. 4) (pp. 187–244). Chicago: University of Chicago Press.

SAS Institute. (1990). *SAS/STAT users guide.* Version 6 (4th ed., Vol. 1). Cary, NC: SAS Institute.

Scott, P., & Yarrow, M. (1965). Manual for experimental procedures for measurement of preschool child's responses to observed distress. Unpublished.

Sears, R. (1951). A theoretical framework for personality and social behavior. *American Psychologist, 6*, 476–478.

Singer, J., & Willett, J. (1991). Modeling the days of our lives: Using survival analysis when designing and analyzing longitudinal studies of duration and the timing of events. *Psychological Bulletin, 110*, 268–290.

Spitzer, R., & Endicott, J. (1977). *The schedule for affective disorders and schizophrenia: Lifetime version.* New York: New York State Psychiatric Institue, Biometrics Research.

Spitzer, R., Endicott, J., & Robins, E. (1978). Research diagnostic criteria. *Archives of General Psychiatry, 15*, 773–782.

Spitzer, R. L., Williams, T. B. W., Gibbon, M., & First, M. B. (1989). *Structured clinical interview for DSM-III-R, nonpatient version.* New York: New York State Psychiatric Institute, Biometrics Research.

Sroufe, L. (1979). The coherence of individual development. *American Psychologist, 34*, 834–841.

Sroufe, L., & Jacobvitz, D. (1989). Diverging pathways, developmental transformations, multiple etiologies and the problem of continuity in development. *Human Development, 32*, 196–203.

Stein, A., Gath, D. H., Bucher, J., Bond, A., Day, A., & Cooper, P. J. (1991). The relationship between post-natal depression and mother–child interaction. *British Journal of Psychiatry, 158*, 46–52.

Tarullo, L. B., DeMulder, E., Martinez, P., & Radke-Yarrow, M. (1994). Dialogues with preadolescents and adolescents: Mother–child interaction patterns in affectively ill and well dyads. *Journal of Abnormal Child Psychology, 22*(1), 33–51.

Tomasson, K., & Kuperman, S. (1990). Bipolar disorder in a prepubescent child. *American Academy of Child and Adolescent Psychiatry, 29*(2), 308–310.

Wachs, T. (1983). The use and abuse of environment in behavior-genetic research. *Child Development, 54*, 396–407.

Webster-Stratton, D., & Hammond, M. (1988). Maternal depression and its relationship to life stress, perceptions of child behavior problems, parenting behaviors, and child conduct problems. *Journal of Abnormal Child Psychology, 16*, 299–315.

Wechsler, D. (1974). *Manual for the Wechsler intelligence scale for children – WISC-R.* New York: Psychological Corporation.

Weintraub, S., Prinz, R. J., & Neale, J. M. (1978). Peer evaluations of competence of children vulnerable to psychopathology. *Journal of Abnormal Child Psychology, 6*(4), 461–473.

Weissman, M. M., Gammon, G. D., John, K., Merikangas, K. R., Warner, V., Prusoff, B. A., & Sholomskas, D. (1987). Children of depressed parents. *Archives of General Psychiatry, 44,* 847–853.

Weissman, M., Gershon, E., Kidd, K., Prusoff, B. A., Leckman, J., Dibble, E., Hamovit, J., Thompson, W., Pauls, D., & Guroff, J. (1984). Psychiatric disorders in the relatives of probands with affective disorders: The Yale–National Institute of Mental Health Study. *Archives of General Psychiatry, 41,* 13–21.

Weissman, M., Kidd, K., & Prusoff, B. A. (1982). Variability in rates of affective disorders in relatives of depressed and normal probands. *Archives of General Psychiatry, 39,* 1397–1403.

Weissman, M. M., & Paykel, E. S. (1974). *The depressed woman: A study of social relationships.* Chicago: University of Chicago Press.

Weissman, M., Prusoff, B., Gammon, G., Merikangas, K., Leckman, J., & Kidd, K. (1984). Psychopathology in the children (age 6–10) of depressed and normal parents. *Journal of the American Academy of Child Psychiatry, 23,* 78–84.

Weissman, M., Wickramaratne, P., Merikangas, K., Leckman, J., Prusoff, B., Caruso, K., Kidd, K., & Gammon, G. (1984). Onset of major depression in early adulthood: Increased familial loading and specificity. *Archives of General Psychiatry, 41,* 1136–1143.

Welner, Z., Welner, A., McCrary, M., & Leonard, M. (1977). Psychopathology in children of inpatients with depression: A controlled study. *Journal of Nervous and Mental Disease, 164,* 408–413.

Werner, E., & Smith R. (1982). *Vulnerable but invincible: A longitudinal study of resilient children and youth.* New York: McGraw-Hill.

Yarrow, M., & Waxler, C. (1978). The emergence and functions of prosocial behaviors in young children. In M. Smart & R. Smart (Eds.), *Infants: Development and relationships* (pp. 77–81). New York: Macmillan.

Zahn-Waxler, C., McKnew, D. H., Cummings, E. M., Davenport, Y. B., & Radke-Yarrow, M. (1984). Problem behaviors and peer interactions of young children with a manic–depressive parent. *American Journal of Psychiatry, 141,* 236–240.

INDEX

211

longitudinal study sample (*cont.*)
   entrance age of parents, 29
   ethnicity, 28
   family composition, 25–27, 29
   number of participants, 29
   socioeconomic level (Hollingshead
      Index), 28–29

major depressive episodes
   in mother, 94
   in offspring, 174
manic–depressive disorder. *See*
   bipolar illness in mother;
      bipolar illness in offspring
manic episodes of mother, effect on
   children, 18, 148
marital discord
   in depressed families, 20, 21, 102,
      104, 106, 107, 108, 109, 110, 112
   in well families, 118
maternal depression. *See* depressed
   mothers
"maturity," of children of bipolar
   mothers, 78
mechanisms of transmission, 9–11, 89–
   90, 98, 166, 180–184, 190–191
mental illness, social meaning of, 188–
   189
middle childhood. *See also*
   prepubertal children's problem
      status
   of children of well and depressed
      mothers, 65–66
modeling, role in child development,
   7
money problems, in depressed
   families, 106, 108, 111, 112, 113
mood disturbances, in depression, 2,
   127
mother–child dyad, as unit of
   analysis, 5, 120, 143, 156–157, 165,
   177, 182–183
mother–child relationship
   affective communication, 127–141,
      137–146

attachment relationship, 139–140,
   156–158
   reciprocal influences, 148–149, 156–
      158, 164
mothering
   conceptualization of. *See*
      conceptualization of mothering
   by depressed women, 14, 22, 131–136
   child development effects, 14–17,
      70–90, 137–139, 182
   predictions from, 139–143
My Family and Friends Interview, as
   social functioning test, 42

narcissistic personality, in depressed
   mothers, 95
negativity, in depressed mothers, 22,
   23, 127, 128, 129, 131, 132, 133, 135,
   137, 143, 144, 162–163, 179
New York Psychiatric Institute, 27
Novel Situation assessment, of
   behavioral inhibition, 37–38

observation of behavior
   child's behavior, 37, 38–39, 45, 130
   mother's interactions with child, 36,
      37, 130
   naturalistic events in apartment, 33–
      35
obsessive–compulsive personality, in
   well and depressed mothers, 95
obsessive personality, 30
"outcome" classifications, of
   children's psychopathology, 91
overinvolvement, of depressed
   mothers. *See* enmeshed
      behavior

paranoia, in depressed mothers, 95
paranoid personality, 30
parental influences on offspring. *See
   also* predictions from first 3 years
   normal and pathological
      development, 7, 147
   revised paradigm, 190–191

psychiatric disorders
family histories of, 19–20, 92–93
in fathers, 107
in offspring of depressed mothers.
See children of depressed
mothers
psychiatric interview assessments
of children of depressed mothers,
38–41
of depressed mothers, 27, 28
psychiatrist, use by depressed
mothers, 43
psychomotor problems
in depressed children, 176, 177
in depression, 2
psychomotor retardation, in
depression, 2
psychopathology
in offspring of depressed mothers.
See under children of depressed
mothers
transmission of, 23–24, 183–184
pubertal children's problem status
bipolar depression in, 175
of well and depressed mothers, 63,
66–67, 72, 74–77, 81–89, 172–173,
176–178
pubertal status (Tanner staging), of
children, 42

racing thoughts, in depressed
children, 177
RDC criteria, use for depressed
mothers, 27
recruitment of participants, 25–27
regression analysis, of data, 47
regulation of toddler, 131–132
rejection, by fathers, 134
relatives, depression in, 1, 19, 93
research design and procedures, 25–
47
conceptual considerations in, 47

sadistic personality, in depressed
mothers, 95

sadness
in depressed children, 150
in depressed mothers, 23, 178
SADS-L. *See* Schedule for Affective
Disorders and Schizophrenia-
Lifetime (SADS-L)
SAS CATMOND procedure, for data
analysis, 46
SAS LIFETEST procedure, for data
analysis, 46
Schedule for Affective Disorders
and Schizophrenia-Lifetime
(SADS-L), use for depressed
parents, 27, 44
schizoid personality, 30
in depressed mothers, 95
schizophrenic mothers, children of, 4
schizotypal personality, 30
in depressed mothers, 95
school performance. *See* academic
performance
SCID. *See* Structure Clinical Interview
for DSM-III-R (SCID)
SCL. *See* Symptom Checklist (SCL)
self-absorption, in depressed mothers,
127
self-blaming, by children of depressed
mothers, 160
self-concept
assessment of, 42
of children of depressed mothers,
70
self-defeating personality, 30
in depressed mothers, 95
self-worth, depression effects on, 2
separation, of depressed parents, 50,
104
separation anxiety, in children of
depressed mothers, 65
sexual molestation, of depressed
family members, 101, 110
shyness, child temperament
assessment of, 154
sibling development (sibling pairs),
factors affecting, 162–163

toddlers
  of depressed parents, 15, 60–61, 64,
    137–142
  of well mothers, 60
transmission, principles of, 183–184
twin studies, on depression, 12

uninvolvement, of depressed mothers,
  23, 131, 132, 133, 134, 136, 141, 146,
  163, 177, 180
unipolar depression in mother
  attachment relationships in, 132–
    133
  family history of psychiatric
    disorders, 19–20, 93
  family stress, 107–108
  marital stress, 107–108
  mothering affective themes, 132
  parenting over time, 134
  personality disorders, 94–96
  problems in offspring, 59–98
  regulation of child by mother, 131–
    132
"used" children, of depressed

mothers, 135, 163
  gender factors, 152

victimization of child, by depressed
  mothers, 152, 159
videotaping, of apartment behavior, 128
violence, of fathers, 131, 134, 168

Wechsler Intelligence Scale for
  Children (WISC & WISC-R),
    use in psychiatric assessments,
      42, 45
Weighted Least Squares (WLS), for
  data analysis, 45–46
well mothers
  development of children of, 59–90
  stress in families of, 117–118
Wilcoxon rank-sum test, use for data
  analysis, 46
Withdrawn Scale, of Child Behavior
  Checklist, daily functioning
  assessment by, 68

Yale longitudinal study, on family
  stress and depression, 20–21